TEACHERS, PERFORMANCE PAY, AND ACCOUNTABILITY

What Education Should Learn From Other Sectors

EPI Series on Alternative Teacher Compensation Systems · No. 1

SCOTT J. ADAMS

JOHN S. HEYWOOD

RICHARD ROTHSTEIN

Preface
Daniel Koretz

Series editors
Sean P. Corcoran and Joydeep Roy

Economic
Policy
Institute

Copyright © 2009
ECONOMIC POLICY INSTITUTE
1333 H Street, NW
Suite 300, East Tower
Washington, DC 20005-4707
www.epi.org
ISBN: 1-932066-38-1

Printed on acid-free paper

Manufactured in the United States of America

Table of Contents

Preface

by Daniel Koretz

Accountability for students' test scores has become the cornerstone of education policy in the United States. State policies that rewarded or punished schools and their staffs for test scores became commonplace in the 1990s. The No Child Left Behind (NCLB) act federalized this approach and made it in some respects more draconian. There is now growing interest in pay for performance plans that would reward or punish individual teachers rather than entire schools. This volume is important reading for anyone interested in that debate.

The rationale for this approach is deceptively simple. Teachers are supposed to increase students' knowledge and skills. Proponents argue that if we manage schools as if they were private firms and reward and punish teachers on the basis of how much students learn, teachers will do better and students will learn more. This straightforward rationale has led to similarly simple policies in which scores on standardized tests of a few subjects dominate accountability systems, to the near exclusion of all other evidence of performance.

It has become increasingly clear that this model is overly simplistic, and that we will need to develop more sophisticated accountability systems. However, much of the debate—for example, arguments about the reauthorization of NCLB—continues as if the current approach were at its core reasonable and that the system needs only relatively minor tinkering. To put this debate on a sensible footing requires that we confront three issues directly.

The first of these critically important issues, addressed in the first section of this volume by Scott Adams and John Heywood, is that the rationale for the current approach misrepresents common practice in the private sector. Pay for performance based on numerical measures actually plays a relatively minor role in the private sector. There are good reasons for this. Economists working on incentives have pointed out for some time that for many occupations (particularly, professionals with complex roles), the available objective measures are seriously incomplete indicators of value to firms, and therefore, other measures, including subjective evaluations, have to be added to the mix.

And that points to the second issue, known as Campbell's Law in the social sciences and Goodhart's Law in economics. In large part because available numerical measures are necessarily incomplete, holding workers accountable for them—without countervailing measures of other kinds—often leads to serious distortions. Workers will often strive to produce what is measured at the expense of what is not, even if what is not measured is highly valuable to the firm. One also often finds that employees "game" the system in various ways that corrupt the performance measures, so that they overstate production even with respect to the goals that are measured. Richard Rothstein's section in this volume shows the ubiquity of this problem and illustrates many of the diverse and even inventive forms it can take. Some distortions are inevitable, even when an accountability system has net positive effects that make it worth retaining. However, the net effects can be negative, and the distortions are often serious enough that they need to be addressed regardless. To disregard this is to pay a great disservice to the nation's children.

The third essential issue is score inflation—increases in scores larger than the improvements in learning warrant—which is the primary form Campbell's Law takes in test-based accountability systems. Many educators and policy makers insist that this is not a serious problem. They are wrong: score inflation is real, common, and sometimes very large.

Three basic mechanisms generate score inflation. The first is gaming that increases aggregate scores by changing the group of students tested—for example, removing students from testing by being lax about truancy or assigning students to special education. The second, which is a consequence of our ill-advised and unnecessary focus on a single cut score (the "proficient" standard), is what many teachers call "the bubble kids problem." Some teachers focus undue effort on students near the cut while reducing their focus on other students well below or above it, because only the ones near the cut score offer the hope of improvement in the numbers that count.

The third mechanism is preparing students for tests in ways that inflates individual students' scores. This mechanism is the least well understood and most controversial, but it can be the most important of the three, creating very large biases in scores. One often hears the argument: "our test is aligned with standards, and it measures important knowledge and skills, so what can be wrong with teaching to it?" This argument is baseless and shows a misunderstanding of both testing and score inflation. Score inflation does not require that the test contain unimportant material. It arises because tests are necessarily small samples of very large domains of achievement. In building a test, one has to sample not only content, but task formats, criteria for scoring, and so on. When this sampling is somewhat predicable—as it almost always is—teachers can emphasize the material most likely to recur, at the expense of other material that is less likely to be tested but that is nonetheless important. The result is scores that overstate mastery of the domain. The evidence is clear that this problem can be very large. There is no space here to discuss this further, but if you are not persuaded, I strongly urge you to read *Measuring Up: What Educational Testing Really Tells Us*, where I explain the basic mechanisms by which this happens and show some of the evidence of the severity of the problem.

My experience as a public school teacher, my years as an educational researcher, and my time as a parent of students in public schools have all persuaded me that we need better accountability in schools. We won't achieve that goal, however, by hiding our heads in the sand. This volume will make an important contribution to sensible debate about more effective approaches.

DANIEL KORETZ is the Henry Lee Shattuck Professor of Education at the Harvard Graduate School of Education, Harvard University, and is a member of the National Academy of Education.

Introduction

by Sean P. Corcoran and Joydeep Roy

With recent research in K-12 education highlighting teacher quality as one of the most important school inputs in educational production, performance-based pay for teachers has been embraced by policy makers across the political spectrum. In the 2008 presidential campaign, for example, both Barack Obama and John McCain touted teacher pay reform as a necessary lever for raising student achievement and closing the achievement gap (Klein 2008; Hoff 2008b).

The use of performance pay in education is not new (Murnane and Cohen 1986). But this latest surge of interest differs from earlier waves in several key respects. First, we have much greater scientific support for investments in teacher quality. Recent research has found that teachers represent the most significant resource schools contribute to academic achievement, a finding that has sharpened policy makers' focus on teacher effectiveness (Hanushek and Rivkin 2006). Second, today's school administrators possess a wealth of achievement measures that can be easily linked to individual teachers. While initially intended for public reporting, these measures have quickly found their way into teacher evaluation and compensation systems. Finally, new and sophisticated statistical models of teacher "value added" have emerged that many believe can be used to accurately estimate teacher effectiveness (Gordon, Kane, and Staiger 2006; Harris 2008).

Proponents of performance pay in education frequently point to the private sector as a model. Where the traditional salary schedule fails to reward excellence in the classroom, it is argued, performance pay is a ubiquitous and powerful tool in the private sector, (Eli Broad recently asserted that he "could not think of any other profession that does not have any rewards for excellence" (Hoff 2008a)). Were schools to explicitly link pay to student achievement (measured through standardized testing), teachers would be incentivized to focus on results, and quality would rise in the long run as high-productivity teachers gravitate into the profession (Hoxby and Leigh 2004).

To be sure, private industry has a longer and richer history of pay-for-performance than public schooling. Not-for-profit and governmental organizations have also experimented with performance accountability systems for decades. But discussions of these experiences are notably absent in the current debate over performance-based pay in education. Is performance pay really ubiquitous among professional workers in the private sector? To what extent are private sector workers compensated based on individual or group measures of productivity? How should performance pay systems be designed? In what types of industries are performance pay systems most effective? How have past performance accountability systems fared in the public sector?

In the first of a series of reports intended to inform the debate over the use of performance-based pay in America's public schools, we compile here two timely and informative papers on performance compensation and evaluation outside of education. In the first, Scott Adams and John Heywood conduct one of the first systematic analyses of the pay-for-performance practices in the private sector. Guided by a simple taxonomy of performance-based pay systems, Adams and Heywood draw upon several large surveys of workers and firms to estimate the overall incidence of performance-based pay in private industry. While they find that periodic "bonus" payments are relatively common (and growing) in the private sector, they represent a very small share of overall compensation and are generally not explicitly tied to simple measures of output. Formulaic payments based on individual productivity measures are rare, particularly among professionals.

In their analysis, Adams and Heywood draw upon several large surveys of workers and firms, including the National Compensation Survey (NCS), National Longitudinal Survey of Youth (NLSY), Panel Study of Income Dynamics (PSID), and National Study of the Changing Workforce (NSCW). While none of these data sources are ideally suited for this task, the conclusions that emerge from their combined analysis are remarkably consistent:

1. Pay tied directly to explicit measures of employee or group output is surprisingly rare in the private sector. For example, in the 2005 NCS, only 6% of private sector workers were awarded regular output-based payments. The incidence is even lower among professionals.

2. "Non production" bonuses, which are less explicitly tied to worker productivity, are common, and their use has grown over time. However, these bonuses represent only a very small share of overall compensation (the median share in the NCS and NLSY ranges from 2% to 3% of overall pay).

3. The incidence and growth of bonus pay is disproportionately concentrated in the finance, insurance, and real estate industries (true in the NCS, NLSY, and NSCW). Additionally, male and non-unionized workers are much more likely to receive performance-based pay.

The low incidence of base or bonus pay tied to individual output does not, of course, imply that private sector compensation is unrelated to job performance. It may be that career *trajectories*—movements into, within, and between firms, for example—are what track worker productivity in the private sector. To the extent this is true, these private sector "career ladders" should be an important consideration for those designing competitive teacher pay systems.

Unfortunately, Adams and Heywood are unable to measure the relationship between private sector career trajectories and individual productivity in their data. But what they do convincingly show is that few professionals are compensated based on formulaic functions of measured output. While many private sector workers earn bonuses, these bonuses represent only a small share of total compensation, and are not necessarily tied to explicit measures of worker output. This result is not surprising. After all, most modern professional work is complex, multi-faceted, and not easily summarized by simple quantitative measures.

In the second part, Richard Rothstein reviews a long history of performance accountability systems in the public and private arena. He begins by recounting the work of social scientists Herbert Simon and Donald Campbell who long ago warned of the problems inherent in measuring public service quality and evaluating complex work with simple quantitative indicators. Through a series of historical examples he highlights countless examples of goal distortion, gaming, and measure corruption in the use of performance evaluation systems. Rothstein concludes that the pitfalls associated with rewarding narrow indicators have led many organizations—including prominent corporations like Wal-Mart and McDonalds—to combine quantitative indicators with broader, more-subjective measures of quality and service.

Rothstein argues that the challenges inherent in devising an adequate system of performance pay in education—appropriately defining and measuring outputs and inputs, for example—surprise many education policy makers, who often blame its failure on the inadequacy of public educators. In fact, corruption and gaming of performance pay systems is not peculiar to public education. The existence of such unintended practices and consequences has been extensively documented in other fields by economists, management theorists, sociologists, and historians. Rothstein's study undertakes the important task of introducing this literature from other fields to scholars of performance incentive systems in education. It reviews evidence from medical care, job training, policing and other human services and shows that overly narrow definitions of inputs and outputs have been pervasive in these sectors' performance measurement systems, often resulting in goal distortion, gaming, or other unintended behaviors. Rothstein also discusses how these problems limit the use of performance incentives in the private sector, and concludes by showing that performance incentives run the risk of subverting the intrinsic motivation of agents in service professions like teaching.

Together, these authors' work provide important context for the implementation of pay-for-performance in education: the incidence of performance pay in the private sector and the experience of performance measurement in both the private and public sectors. These studies offer lessons which will be crucial in the debate over whether performance pay is suited to education, and how we think about designing and implementing such a system. Later papers in this series will review the history and experiments with performance pay systems in U.S. education, critically analyze some of the most important merit pay systems currently in use by school districts across the country, suggest alternative frameworks for teacher compensation, and discuss how teachers themselves feel about pay-for-performance.

Bibliography

Gordon, Robert, Thomas J. Kane, and Douglas O. Staiger. 2006. *Identifying Effective Teachers Using Performance on the Job*. Policy Report, The Hamilton Project. Washington, D.C.: Brookings Institution.

Hanushek, Eric A., and Steven G. Rivkin. 2006. "Teacher Quality," in E. A. Hanushek, and F. Welch, eds., *Handbook of the Economics of Education*. Elsevier, 2006, pp. 1051-1078.

Harris, Douglas N. 2008. "The Policy Uses and 'Policy Validity' of Value-Added and Other Teacher Quality Measures," in D. H. Gitomer, ed., *Measurement Issues and the Assessment of Teacher Quality*. Thousand Oaks, Calif.: SAGE Publications.

Hoff, David J. 2008a. Teacher-pay issue is hot in DNC discussions. *Education Week*. August 25.

Hoff, David J. 2008b. McCain and Obama tussle on education. *Education Week*. October 22.

Hoxby, Caroline M., and Andrew Leigh. 2004. Pulled away or pushed out? Explaining the decline of teacher aptitude in the United States. *American Economic Review*. Vol. 94, pp. 236-40.

SEAN P. CORCORAN is an assistant professor at New York University Steinhardt School of Culture, Education, and Human Development.

JOYDEEP ROY is an economist at the Economic Policy Institute. His areas of focus include economics of education, education policy, and public and labor economics.

PART I

Performance Pay in the U.S. Private Sector
Concepts, Measurement, and Trends

by Scott J. Adams and John S. Heywood

1.1

Introduction

Recent research in K-12 education has identified teacher quality as one of the most important school inputs in educational production. At the same time, many of the nation's school districts—and in particular its large urban school districts—are finding it increasingly difficult to attract and retain highly effective teachers. These facts have coalesced into a renewed effort to improve the quality of the teaching force. To this end, education reformers have proposed relaxing the traditional "single salary schedule" used in teaching in favor of merit-based pay (Podgursky and Springer 2007). Such merit-based proposals often incorporate pay-for-performance aligned with measurable outcomes, such as student test scores (Staiger, Gordon, and Kane 2006).

How teachers should be paid is part of a broader inquiry into how public sector workers should be compensated (Belman and Heywood 1996). Government is under increased pressure to improve workforce productivity and has often borrowed from the private sector in creating incentives that reward workers for performance. This was explicit in the creation of a merit pay system for the Departments of Homeland Security and Defense. It was evident in the Bush administration's call to eliminate the General Schedule pay system in favor of pay for performance (Lee 2005), and Medicare's consideration of implementing performance pay for physicians (Casalino et al. 2007).

Proponents of performance pay in teaching frequently point to the private sector as a model, and common wisdom suggests that private firms make greater use of performance pay than the public sector. For example, speaking recently about teacher compensation, philanthropist Eli Broad noted, "I can't think of any other profession that doesn't have any rewards for excellence" (Hoff 2008). In fact, there have been few systematic investigations into the incidence of pay-for-performance in the private sector, and in particular its use in professional occupations. We seek to fill this gap, identifying the extent of, and recent trends in, U.S. private sector performance pay practices.

We recognize that there is wide variation in what can be deemed "performance pay," and begin with a fairly detailed taxonomy of performance-oriented pay practices. Following this, we provide a selective review of the literature in employment relations and the economics of personnel, summarizing what is known about the potential and pitfalls associated with broad types of performance pay. We emphasize that these plans differ widely in their effects on performance, motivation, and unintended consequences, and establish that no single type flourishes in all circumstances. It remains far from clear that performance pay routinely drives the right worker behavior or necessarily increases productivity. We show that both the nature of the job and also technology influence the pay design that has the best chance of generating positive outcomes.

Next, we introduce a variety of data sources in order to examine the prevalence of performance pay in the U.S. private sector. We find that relatively few workers have pay that varies in a direct formulaic way with their productivity, and that the share of such workers is probably declining. We show that while many workplaces can identify something called a "bonus," it often does not meet the test of actually being regular performance-related pay. The share of workers who have a bonus that is, indeed, tied to performance, often through a judgmental evaluation process rather by formula, has grown, but even these workers remain concentrated in specific occupations and industries. In total, the evidence suggests that the expansion in performance pay has been largely a non-union, male phenomenon concentrated among managers and professionals and in finance, insurance, and real estate.

Types of Performance Pay

This section describes a variety of deviations from *fixed* time rates of pay that, as a group, we label performance pay. We emphasize that not all deviations from fixed time rates are automatically performance pay. One-time bonus pay given across the board in lieu of a more traditional wage increase may be variable pay, but it is certainly not performance pay. Performance pay requires that earnings be linked to some measure of performance. At the same time, when time rates explicitly depend on performance, they should not be viewed as fixed. Yet even such a broad label as deviations from fixed time rates based on performance can be misleading as a fixed hourly wage may still have a performance standard for continued employment (Lazear 2000). However, we persist in the label both because of its common usage in the literature, and also because we will be explicit in separating the various types of incentive schemes. We will use the resulting taxonomy of the types of incentive schemes to narrow the discussion to those most relevant when considering the translation to the public sector. The purpose will be to emphasize both the potential benefits of performance pay and the well-recognized negative side effects.

At its most basic, the adoption of performance pay is intended to align the interests of workers with the goals of the enterprises for which they work (Kessler and Purcell 1992). For private-sector enterprises, the ultimate goal of the enterprise is increased profit, but translating that goal into performance pay may take many forms. A simple formulaic sharing of profit can often create only very weak alignment because the individual worker's contribution to overall profit is negligible (Heywood and Jirjahn 2006). Thus, the object is to find a more immediate measure of the worker's contribution to profit. While that value-added may be difficult to exactly measure, it may be related to more easily identified indicators such as the individual's or group's contribution to output, quality, or sales. The extent to which these indicators are correlated with the worker's value-added plays a crucial role in determining the success of the performance pay scheme as outlined in the next section.

We modify a taxonomy developed by Milkovich and Widgor (1991) to categorize the varieties of performance pay. They put all performance pay plans into a two-by-two matrix with every plan characterized by the level at which performance was being measured (group vs. individual) and whether the resulting pay increment was permanent (added to base vs. one time). Obviously, there can remain some variation within such a matrix. A group level plan can measure the performance of small work team, a portion of an assembly operation, an entire plant, or all employees in the firm. Also, a particular firm may adopt an overall plan that includes elements that cross the lines of the matrix. For example, following an appraisal, a worker may receive both a salary increment and one-time bonus. Even more dramatically, the same employee may participate in both individual plans and a group plan, say, both a merit pay scheme and profit sharing.

To this original matrix we add a third dimension. In addition to the level of measurement and whether the increment adds to base, it is crucial to distinguish formulaic from judgmental performance measurement (Baker, Jensen, and Murphy 1988). This is not an issue of whether personnel managers are accurate in their assessments. Instead, it identifies whether or not performance is easily measured, observed by all, and agreed upon in advance. Thus, formulaic measures are characterized by a low degree of supervisory discretion. These measures may be either output-based measures or input-based measures. Formulaic output measures include number of units produced, the profit rate, tolerance as a measure of quality, and the value of sales. Formulaic input measures could include attendance, number of sales calls, or specific job training undertaken. Any of these measures, input or output, can be the right or wrong measure to drive the appropriate behavior, but they are easily measured, and their realizations are subject to relatively little debate. As will be shown, these formulaic plans do not cover a large share of the workforce. Judgmental measures entail a substantial degree of discretion usually taking place in a performance evaluation from a supervisor (e.g., evaluation of a worker's cooperativeness or ability to meet goals). Again, judgmental is not pejorative in this context and may be the appropriate way to identify the contributions of workers with many activities who interact with others frequently and cannot be tied to an objective measure.[1]

Thus, each of the major types of performance pay can be seen as roughly fitting into this three-way taxonomy. Piece rates and commissions that reward workers for their units produced or sales are schemes that do not add to base, are individual, and formulaic. Typical merit pay plans add to base, are individual but judgmental as they are based on a performance evaluation. Gain sharing and profit sharing do not add to base, are group and formulaic. Typical bonuses may be group or individual, do not add to base, and are often judgmental based on an appraisal. At its most muddled, assignment of a more lucrative sales territory or promotion to sales manager is often based on past sales success. Here a formulaic measurement may be seen as adding to base even as the payment method is a commission.

How these examples fit in the taxonomy demonstrates again the point that not all forms of variable pay are performance pay. Thus, a separate payment given in place of employer-sponsored benefits such as waived employer-provided health insurance may be variable from year to year, but is not tied to worker performance. Similarly, a hiring bonus paid to a new employee upon agreeing to work for a firm cannot be related to their performance once on that job. A union contract may include both a settlement over salary and one-time bonus figures, but these are simply a way of dividing payment into a base and one-time contribution, with the latter not related to performance.

While these and other forms of variable pay should not be identified as performance pay, some performance pay schemes obviously do not involve variable pay. Thus, every worker may be paid a salary, but the annual increments and so the variations in pay at any point in time may reflect the performance measurement. Less obviously, pay within grade may be similar, but promotion between grades may be based on performance measurement. This might lead to a further theoretical division between performance pay that is absolute versus that which is relative. In the latter, the better workers are promoted, made partner, or given tenure. The reward is based on a comparison across workers not on any *a priori* standard. Certainly, economists have long recognized that such workplace tournaments are designed to elicit greater performance and effort (Lazear and Rosen 1981). Yet, tournaments are often difficult to uncover in the data, and even the losers in a tournament have been part of the scheme although they have no resulting pay increment. As important as such tournaments may be in some workplaces, few are recommending that teachers' salaries depend upon such a scheme. Instead, it is more common to tie earnings to an absolute measure of performance such as standardized student achievement.

The fact that variable pay and performance pay are overlapping but not identical is critical in examining the existing data on the extent of performance pay. As we will show, many "bonuses" identified in common data sources are often variable pay but not performance pay. Some circumstances identified as time rates may still have critical elements of performance pay.

Figure A presents a summary matrix that overlays our emphasis on formulaic versus judgmental measurement on the original two-way distinction of Milkovich and Wigdor (1991). We have filled in various types of performance pay schemes as appropriate. The resulting framework provides the variation in performance pay to discuss positive and negative aspects of the different schemes.

FIGURE A Matrix of performance pay types

			Level of measurement	
			Individual	*Group*
Relationship to base	Adds	*Formulaic*	Some promotions, sales territory assignment	
		Judgmental	Merit pay plans	Small group incentives
	Doesn't add	*Formulaic*	Piece rates, commissions	Gain sharing, Profit sharing
		Judgmental	Bonus tied to appraisal	Team bonus

Potential and Pitfalls for Performance Pay

This section reviews aspects of performance pay around three large categories: formulaic individual performance pay, judgmental individual performance pay, and group-level performance pay.

Formulaic individual performance pay

An individual-level scheme offers the tightest connection between individual variations in performance and variations in pay. Hence, individual performance pay based on formulaic measures of output is usually thought to provide very strong incentives for workers. First, workers are induced to exert high effort. Second, high-productivity workers sort into jobs where they are rewarded (Lazear 1986).

Yet, the trade-off between insurance and incentives acts to limit the extent of performance pay. If a worker's performance depends not only on effort but also on random outside influences (technology, weather, health problems, and performance indicators that depend on supervisors' idiosyncratic perceptions), performance pay introduces income risk (Milgrom and Roberts 1992). When performance pay involves income risk, risk-averse workers must receive compensating differentials. The stronger the link between performance and pay, the higher must be the differential. Hence, the employer will limit the intensity of the incentive scheme to reduce the compensating differential. This reasoning yields a clear prediction. The higher the variance of (measured) performance, the weaker the link between pay and performance. However, empirical tests of this prediction obtain mixed results (Prendergast 2002), suggesting that factors beyond the trade-off between insurance and incentives influence the design of performance pay.

An employer will also limit the intensity of performance pay if workers are subject to a limited liability (or wealth) constraint. Optimal incentives require that workers are both rewarded for good performance and punished for bad. Yet, with a binding limited liability constraint, workers cannot be punished for bad performance. That is, they would never have to "pay" the firm. Thus, incentives to exert effort can only be provided by higher rewards for good performance. This generates a rent for the workers. The employer faces a trade-off between limited liability rents and incentives.

The higher the effort induced by the incentives, the higher a worker's rent. Workers queue for jobs with these rents, while employers are reluctant to invest in creating such jobs (Jirjahn 2006).

Performance pay also entails important dynamic aspects (Gibbons 1987). Workers withhold both effort and productivity-enhancing ideas in the current period because they fear an increase in performance standards after a period of good performance. Such output restrictions will increase if negative group norms evolve and workers exert peer pressure on colleagues who exercise high effort (Levine 1992). A precondition for the fear of increasing performance standards is that the employer cannot credibly commit to a fixed performance standard. Several (partially opposing) ways to alleviate or overcome this problem have been suggested. Short-term workers are less likely to fear increasing standards because they are not affected by a future increase in performance standards (Milgrom and Roberts 1992). More importantly, cooperative employer–employee relations characterized by workers' involvement in the implementation, design, and change of incentives schemes may engender the trust and fairness that makes performance pay feasible. Heywood, Huebler, and Jirjahn (1998) suggest this as the explanation behind their evidence that piece rates are more common in German workplaces with works councils. Kim (1999) argues the same thing, finding that the agreement and involvement of unions makes gain-sharing plans more successful.

Even without fear of increased performance targets, individual-based performance pay may not be appropriate for work characterized by multitasking (Holmstrom and Milgrom 1991; Baker 1992). In these situations workers must allocate their efforts across different productive tasks. If the employer rewards only one task, or a few tasks, workers have an incentive to cut back on those productive tasks for which they are not rewarded. These behaviors include helping colleagues (Drago and Garvey 1996), maintaining equipment, cultivating customer goodwill, striving for quality, and reducing chances of workplace injury (Freeman and Kleiner 2005).

Interestingly, even if the employer identifies all the tasks appropriately and knows the relevant weights in its objective function, the resulting performance pay scheme may still not generate the right allocation of effort across tasks. In response to such a performance pay scheme, the worker retains an incentive to allocate more time to the easiest (least costly in terms of effort) tasks. MacDonald and Marx (2001) emphasize that this "adverse specialization" can be completely overcome only with the ability to write a performance pay contract that accounts for the costs associated with each of the activities identified in the performance pay scheme. Knowledge of the workers' effort costs may be rare, and absent this information MacDonald and Marx argue that little or no specific compensation should be awarded for each task.

In addition to cutting back on productive behaviors or adversely specializing, performance pay can cause workers to actually increase unproductive influence activities. Thus, Heywood and Jirjahn (2006) argue that piece rate workers in Germany who directly participate in investment decisions push for investments that allow increased output rather than increased efficiency.

These problems may all be seen as what Kerr (1975) called the "folly of rewarding A while hoping for B," and recent examples are myriad. Dun and Bradstreet faced large legal costs and customer resentment following a performance pay scheme that caused brokers to provide customers fraudulent information in order to make sales. Sears created an individual performance pay plan that caused their mechanics to exaggerate the repairs that customers needed for their automobiles in an effort to increase individual earnings (see Gibbons 1998 for more on these two examples). In the public sector, Asch (1990) found that military recruiters paid by their number of recruits signed up a lower quality of recruit. Cragg (1997) examined the performance pay scheme of the Job Partnership Training Act that rewarded trainers for higher levels of wages and employment for trainees. He found that the performance rewards created cream skimming in which those trained were the least likely to need training and were those who would have done the best in the labor market even absent training. Eberts, Hollenberg, and Stone (2002) compare two similar secondary schools in Michigan, one of which explicitly rewards teachers for retention and one of which retains a traditional earnings plan without merit pay. They found that the first school successfully increased retention rates relative to the second, but it also had an increased rate of course failure, lower average attendance, and no increase in achievement. While the rewarded performance measure increased, the ultimate success of the school fell. Finally, physicians believe the proposed performance pay associated with Medicare will result in their avoiding high risk cases further increasing racial and socioeconomic disparities in health care delivery (Casalino et al. 2007). In each of these cases, the measure of performance identified in the pay scheme fails to capture all the dimensions of worker productivity.

Judgmental individual performance pay

One possibility to alleviate the problems outlined in the previous paragraphs is to have supervisors make comprehensive judgments about the productivity of individual workers. This more complete assessment of productivity could evaluate helping others, learning new skills, participating effectively in groups, enhancing quality, or cultivating good relations with customers. Indeed, Brown and Heywood (2005) show that such formal performance appraisal becomes more likely when jobs are complex and multifaceted. Their Australian data confirm that formal appraisal for non-managerial workers occurs where workers have greater control over the pace and variety of tasks. Such control allows wider variance in performance increasing the benefits from appraisal (and its link to pay).

But using supervisor evaluations for performance pay can generate its own folly. The difficult process of evaluating workers has spawned concern with validity, reliability, and freedom from bias. The early focus was primarily on the role of the supervisor and the nature of rating scales. Researchers identified common errors made by supervisors, such as halo effects (a favorable overall rating based on outstanding performance in only a single duty), central tendency bias (rating all employees close to the scale mid-point, irrespective of performance), and recency effects (placing too much emphasis on recent performance) (Milkovich and Newman 2002; Lewin and Mitchell 1995). In addition, there is the recognized tendency to give greater weight over time to those criteria that can be most easily and objectively measured. Thus, what begins as a more comprehensive evaluation involving supervisory latitude can degenerate into something that rewards only one or a few of the dimensions of productivity.

More dramatically, the prejudices of the evaluator may enter the performance pay process. Elvira and Town (2001) confirm that the race of subordinates influences super-visors' performance evaluations. They found that white supervisors of both white and nonwhite subordinates typically give whites better ratings than nonwhites, even after controlling for productivity and demographic variables. This result is more disquieting when the evaluations form the basis of pay decisions. Workers with the same productivity would have different earnings by race but also would have supervisory evaluations supporting the differences. Such an implication fits with a broader perspective that in less formulaic performance pay systems that depend on judgment, worker characteristics and the composition of the workforce play greater roles in determining compensa-tion (Elvira and Graham 2002). Indeed, Heywood and O'Halloran (2005) found that measured racial discrimination is largest among those workers receiving bonuses (typically the result of a judgmental evaluation) and smallest among those being paid according to a formulaic output measure (such as a piece rate) with that for time-rate workers in the middle.

Added to the possibilities of honest mistakes and of prejudice is the possibility that performance measures will be strategically manipulated. Employers may underreport performance to save on wages (Prendergast 1999). Moreover, individual supervisors may use their discretion to reward only subordinates who provide private services or goods (Laffont 1990; Prendergast and Topel 1996). These services include flattery or loyalty to the superior's career concerns. Alternatively, the superior may rate all employees highly to demonstrate to those further up the hierarchy his or her outstanding managerial skills. A less productive superior may even favor unproductive subordinates to protect himself or herself from being replaced by productive subordinates (Friebel and Raith 2004). Also, a subordinate may strategically engage in influence activities that result in a positive evaluation but not necessarily in increased performance (Milgrom and Roberts 1988). Thus, in Prendergast's (1993) theory of "yes men," superiors favor proposals from subordinates that mirror their own opinions. This creates incentives for subordinates to make just such proposals. Strategic manipulation may be reduced if reputation concerns matter and interactions are long-term (Baker, Gibbons, and Murphy 1994). Additionally, the presence of organized labor in the appraisals may help with enforcement and reduce the incentives to manipulate the process.

This long list of "perverse incentives" (Lewin and Mitchell 1995) has some researchers suggesting alternative procedures. One such procedure is 360-degree appraisal which Edwards and Ewen (1996) show to be less susceptible to prejudice, bias, and strategic behavior. These appraisals typically involve not a single supervisor evaluating a subordinate but the participation of all those around a particular worker—above, below, and parallel. Yet Antonioni (1996) has suggested that such appraisals are typically resource intensive, applied only to managers, and are often intended as a developmental rather than an evaluative tool. Nonetheless, Brett and Atwater (2001) argue that a 360-degree appraisal has been associated with improved performance.

Even given the potential of such alternatives, we suggest that judgmental performance evaluations cannot always avoid the folly of "rewarding A while hoping for B." Indeed, the sum of practical concerns associated with operating a valid and reliable performance appraisal system and then using it to create a merit pay scheme was what caused Pfeffer's quip quoted earlier that all merit pay schemes "share two attributes: they absorb vast amounts of management time and resources, and make everyone unhappy."

Despite the problems associated with individual performance pay (both formulaic and judgmental), their growth has been noted, and that growth has been shown to be associated with increasing inequality in U.S. earnings (Lemieux et al. 2007). This association may be evidence of a continued decline in internal labor markets and a movement, however gradual, toward spot markets. Cannon et al. (2000) present related evidence of growing wage dispersion across occupations within establishments but of decreasing earnings dispersion within occupations across similar firms. While the first effect may be the influence of skill-biased technical change, the authors attribute the second effect to a decompression of within establishment earnings in which internal hierarchies and pay equity considerations give way to "meeting the market" for particular occupations, a move toward spot labor markets. Yet, it would be wrong to conclude that from the combined evidence of Lemieux et al. (2007) and Cannon et al. (2000) that performance pay of all types is necessarily associated with eroding internal labor markets. Promotions and merit pay exercises that increase base earnings may be important parts of an internal labor market. While variable performance pay may be more likely to reflect a diminished role for the internal labor market, even this is not uniform. Geddes and Heywood (2003) suggest that while piece rates were associated with more nearly spot labor markets (low tenure, part-time status, and so on), sales workers earning commissions were less likely to exhibit the characteristics of spot labor markets.

Before leaving the case of individual-based performance pay (be it formulaic or judgmental) it is worth considering the case of multiple supervisors. It has often been argued that public sector workers have to serve many masters (Burgess 2003). Thus, each principal will reward the activities he or she is interested in and punish the activities he or she is not interested in. Obviously, this creates a negative externality to other principals with different interests. The aggregate marginal incentive for each activity can be shown to be decreasing in the number of principals because of the externality. Dixit (1997 and 2002) explores circumstances in which the externality can and cannot be internalized but emphasizes the difficulty of driving appropriate worker behavior in this circumstance.

Group level rewards

In moving to a consideration of group level performance pay, we recognize that much of the work of employees is not theirs alone. They work in teams with interdependent worker productivity producing a joint product. Often the individual contribution cannot be accurately determined. Individual schemes in this context are either fruitless or counter-productive as they detract from team performance by increasing the effort cost of cooperating (Milgrom and Roberts 1990). In such cases, replacing individual rewards with team (group) rewards can be sensible. At the most extreme in terms of group size, profit sharing stands as an ideal that aligns the interests of private-sector workers with their firms.

The well-known difficulty with group rewards is that they encourage members of the group to free-ride on the effort of others. The larger the group, the greater is the free-riding. The optimal group compensation scheme depends on how easy it is to measure team productivity and the size of the team. Thus, group schemes become increasingly complex to design and monitor as measurement becomes difficult and the size grows (Holmstrom 1982). While particular technologies or forms of group behavior can help reduce the increased free-riding associated with greater size (Fitzroy and Kraft 1987; Adams 2006), theory nonetheless suggests that group schemes, including profit sharing should have minimal impact as a direct incentive to elicit greater effort.

Despite the predicted lack of success generated by free-riding, team rewards and profit sharing are frequently used and are often associated with higher productivity (Bhargara 1994; Cable and Wilson 1989; Estrin et al. 1997; Hueber 1993; Kruse 1992; Wadhwani and Wall 1990). Thus, while the expectation that linking pay and performance can increase worker productivity stands at the center of personnel economics, the causation in the case of profit sharing remains among the least obvious. This may be a result of its ability to create positive work-group norms and enforce greater effort through peer pressure (Kandel and Lazear 1992). Thus, the free-rider problem is overcome by the desire not to let coworkers down. Yet, importantly, this peer pressure can be a negative job attribute that limits the optimal extent of group rewards. Freeman, Kruse, and Blasi (2004) provide survey evidence that profit sharing (a large group reward) does encourage workers to act against shirking behavior and thus reduce the tendency to free-ride. Yet, they show that profit sharing induces worker actions against shirkers only if employees have a very positive view of management–employee relations.

Profit sharing may also change employment relations so as to create greater investment in worker training, and it is this training that improves productivity (Azfar and Danninger 2001; Parent 2004). Further, it may be the ability of profit sharing to reduce turnover and separations that helps generate productivity by creating longer-term employment relations (Weitzman 1984).

Despite the potential importance of profit sharing as a form of performance pay, we note that there is no easy public sector equivalent. Very few of the "products" from governments sell in competitive markets, and it seems doubtful that profit maximization is an appropriate objective for governmental programs that often provide public goods or have redistributive objectives. Thus, while we will present some evidence on the private sector incidence of profit sharing, we will consciously avoid a detailed examination.

Smaller group rewards can be appropriate for individual teams and are often thought to be an element in workplace transformation (Cooke 1994). There exists some interesting evidence that such rewards increase the productivity of those who were otherwise toward the bottom in terms of initial productivity but leave largely unchanged the productivity of those initially with higher productivity (Hansen 1997). Thus, aggregate group productivity increases by bringing up the bottom of the group distribution and reducing the variance in productivity.

Unfortunately, few (if any) large scale U.S. micro data sources provide information on the use of smaller group incentives together with the use of other forms of performance pay. As a consequence, their use will be largely unexplored in this data analysis. Thus, this study mainly (but not entirely) focuses on the use of individual level performance pay.

1.4

Measuring Performance Pay
U.S. Incidence and Trends

In reviewing a variety of data sources to determine the incidence of performance pay, no single source provides a definitive answer. The complex variations in both the concept of performance pay and the differences in actual survey questions require an examination of multiple sources. In this section, we review the data of others and draw our own in an effort to provide a well-rounded overview. We emphasize that each of the data sources provides only a partial answer to the question of what is the prevalence of performance pay. The units of observations differ, the sample designs differ, and definitions of key variables differ. This limits us from drawing strong cross-survey conclusions such as "in four of five surveys the incidence of performance pay is less than 20%." Nonetheless, some general patterns, even if blurry around the edges, will emerge. We emphasize that the data sources we examine represent among the most commonly examined national data sources used by economists interested in the issue of performance pay.

Large firm survey data

The Center for Effective Organizations at the University of Southern California regularly surveys major corporations on their pay practices. Lawler (2003) presents the results over the period from 1987 to 2002. The 2002 survey was sent to all firms in the Fortune 1,000 and a total of 149 responded. While these firms were somewhat larger than the remainder of the Fortune 1,000 firms, they were comparable to the firms that answered the survey in previous years. The surveys were sent to CEOs asking that they complete it or turn it over to someone knowledgeable about pay practices. The results provide a time series on the practices of the largest of the large U.S. corporations.

The most relevant portion of the survey for our purposes asks about the incidence of specific pay for performance practices. For each of seven practices, the firms report the percent of their workers that are covered by indicating one of five quintiles or zero or 100%. **Table 1** summarizes the reports from 1987 to 2002 by showing the share of firms that indicate that more than 60% of their workers are covered (that is, they report either of the upper two quintiles or 100%).

The practice with the largest coverage is "non-monetary recognition," which one hesitates to call performance pay. This practice includes publicity, dinners, or gifts for

TABLE 1 The percent of major corporations (Fortune 1,000) that have more than 60% of their employees covered by various performance rewards

Type of reward	1987	1990	1993	1996	1999	2002
Individual incentives	5%	13%	12%	21%	25%	33%
Group or team incentives	--	6	11	12	20	20
Gain sharing	2	2	7	7	11	14
Profit sharing	30	33	33	42	35	42
Stock ownership plan	44	47	50	52	51	55
Stock option plan	--	--	13	18	24	24
Non-monetary recognition awards	--	49	49	53	61	56

Note: Blank entries indicate that questions about that type of performance pay were not asked in the relevant year.

Source: Center for Effective Organizations as reported by Lawler (2003).

those individuals or groups who have performed well. In 2002, a total of 56% of the surveyed firms indicate that more than 60% of their workers are covered (eligible) for such recognition. The practice with the second largest coverage is stock ownership plans. These plans enable employees to buy their employer's stock. The stock is often held in trust until employees quit or retire. In 2002, 55% of the firms surveyed indicated that more than 60% of employees were covered. Before concluding that this is performance pay, one would want to know the extent to which, if any, the employer subsidizes the stock purchases. Also, if subsidized, is this primarily a retirement savings vehicle the value of which does not vary with the performance of the individual, group, or firm? Put differently, if all workers independent of firm and individual performance have the ability to purchase stock for retirement, this should not be identified as performance pay. Owning stock may align the interests of workers with firms, increasing loyalty and reducing turnover, but not everything that aligns interests should necessarily be identified as performance pay. Finally, it is also worth noting that profit sharing, stock ownership plans, and stock options do not have ready public sector equivalents.

Thus, the attention from these surveys should be focused on the use of individual and group performance pay. These are identified in the survey as "bonuses or other financial compensation tied to short- or long-term performance." The largest gain in coverage of any practice is in individual incentives. A third of the firms now cover more than 60% of their employees compared with only 5% of firms in 1987. Perhaps more dramatically, and not shown in Table 1, 62% of firms reported in 1987 that 20% or less of their workers received individual incentives and by 2002 this fell by more than half to only 28% of firms. In 2002, the median firm fell in the upper portion of the 21-40% coverage quintile. Moreover, that is also the modal quintile.

Lawler (2003, 46) summarizes that "organizations are doing more to tie individual performance to pay, and doing it in ways that use variable pay." This is likely correct for this sample, but the wording of the question allows for both "other financial compensation" and longer-term evaluation, leaving open the likelihood that not all of the performance pay is variable and that it may, instead, add to base. In addition, the survey obviously makes no distinction between performance that is determined by formula or by judgment. More generally, left unmeasured is the frequency with which covered employees receive performance pay and the portion of their pay that is actually performance related when they do receive it. Nonetheless, the country's very largest firms clearly appear to be making greater use of individual performance pay, but it still remains far from universal even in this sample.[2]

It is perhaps surprising that group-based incentives have not grown as dramatically as individual incentives given the increased use of teams. Also interesting is the growth in gain sharing. Often associated with unionized workforces (Kim 1999), these programs share productivity gains with workers and have increased from relatively uncommon to 20% of firms saying they cover more than 60% of their workers. This growth may reflect a broader international trend that union leaders increasingly see the need to make performance pay transparent and fair as part of their mission (van het Karr and Grunell 2002; Heywood 2005).

The firm survey presents a coverage rate within the firm that may not be well correlated with the role that performance pay plays in the broader economy. Not only are there the issues mentioned above involving the regularity and intensity of the payments, but also the survey reports only on a select sample of the largest U.S. firms. As performance pay involves substantial setup costs and updating costs, it is more apt to be found in larger firms (Heywood and Jirjahn 2006). Alternative methods of determining incidence include examining survey data from individual workers and using broader establishment surveys. We will again be facing important issues of definition and measurement.

BLS Establishment Survey data

As part of broad National Compensation Survey projects, the Bureau of Labor Statistics (BLS) creates the Employment Cost Index (ECI) that collects and codes the components of labor costs. The objective of the ECI is to measure changes in the "price" (not the earnings) of labor (Ruser 2001). In doing so, they survey sample jobs and code them as "incentive pay" jobs when "regular performance-related payments are *directly* related to the employee's individual or group output." Most of the payments are related to individual performance, and many of the jobs identified as receiving incentive pay also receive time rates as well. This definition of incentive pay depends heavily upon there being a formulaic relationship between a measure of output (or productivity) and earnings.

Incentive pay coded this way explicitly excludes most bonuses, employee-of-the-year awards and, indeed, any payments at the discretion of the employer (whether tied to performance or not). The most important exclusion from our point of view is performance pay dependent upon a supervisory appraisal. Each of these excluded types of variable payment (including but not limited to performance pay linked to appraisal) are identified as "non-production bonuses" by the BLS and are discussed in more detail shortly. In the meantime, note that while many of the occupations identified closely with the BLS definition of incentive pay can be anticipated (e.g., sales workers), there are few surprises. For instance, a substantial share of optometrists receives incentive pay—earnings linked directly to number of exams completed (Barkume and Moehrle 2004). We also emphasize that those jobs identified as incentive pay jobs are far less likely to receive non-production bonuses (Barkume 2004).

While the BLS incentive pay definition is narrow and largely limits itself to piece rates and commissions, it is nonetheless instructive as it is based on a very large survey of jobs and employers rather than being dependent on the relatively few individuals in worker survey data. We examine the resulting incidence of incentive pay over the 12 years for which it is available from 1995 to 2006. Using a special tabulation of the incidence by quarter for private-sector workers, a simple average of the eight quarters within each two-year period is calculated and presented as the first column in Table 2. In short, only a weak secular trend emerges. If pushed, there may be a slight decline over the years. Such a decline matches what we will identify in the individual level survey data on piece rates and commissions. The incidence in **Table 2** was 6.7% in 1995-96 and fell to 6.0% in 2005-06.

The remaining columns of Table 2 repeat the exercise for various broad occupational groups.[3] Professionals and related groups have little formulaic incentive pay, and the incidence remains constant at around 1.3%. The incidence in management and finance seems to be near the overall average, but it does seem to have increased very substantially over the time frame. As the use of commissions might suggest,

TABLE 2 BLS ECI data on incidence of incentive payments for private industry workers

	Total	Other profess- ional	Mgmt.	Sales	Clerical	Service	Con- struct/ Primary	Install, maintain, repair	Pro- duction	Trans- port
1995-96	6.70%	1.38%	5.13%	22.59%	1.83%	3.15%	1.28%	11.36%	7.85%	11.92%
1997-98	6.46	1.30	5.36	23.09	1.52	4.38	1.20	13.53	5.48	8.71
1999-2000	6.13	1.30	5.33	21.10	2.19	4.58	1.24	11.15	4.38	9.08
2001-02	6.44	1.20	9.25	21.98	2.34	3.00	1.98	11.85	5.03	8.79
2003-04	6.38	1.29	9.48	21.55	3.01	2.75	1.75	10.25	5.43	9.35
2005-06	6.00	1.30	8.24	19.95	3.59	2.21	1.96	11.05	4.66	8.84

Note: These are aggregated from quarterly data provided by a special tabulation from the Bureau of Labor Statistics. Each number represents the percentage of workers in the particular industry in jobs where "regular performance-related payments are *directly* related to the employee's individual or group output."

Source: Authors' calculations from Bureau of Labor Statistics data.

sales workers have a very high incidence of formulaic incentive payments—nearly four times the overall average. Interestingly, there is a suggestion that the incidence among sales workers is decreasing over the time period. Clerical workers have below average incidence of incentive pay, but it appears to be modestly increasing. Service workers also have a below-average incidence of incentive pay but with no clear secular pattern. Construction and primary occupations (fishing, mining, farming and forestry) have a very low incidence of incentive pay, routinely below 2%. Installation, maintenance, and repair occupations (including Lazear's (2000) iconic windshield replacement case study) have a higher-than-average incidence but again without a strong secular pattern. Production occupations seem to have roughly similar incidence to the overall average, but there does appear to be a decline in incidence over the period. The transportation occupations have a higher than average incidence that also seems to have declined modestly over the period.

The conclusions from the BLS incentive data are first that the overall incidence is small, with only about one worker in 15 receiving compensation from a formulaic (and largely) individual performance pay scheme. Second, the incidence has been declining modestly over the last 12 years. Third, evidence within the detailed occupational groups shows that the decline, while not dramatic, has been uneven. Within this decline, there exist much larger declines in traditional high incidence occupations like sales workers and transport operatives.[4] At the same time, there is surprisingly large growth in the incidence of formulaic pay schedules for managerial and finance workers. The incidence in this group has grown from below the overall average to above the overall average. Such growth will match the picture from the individual data of the National Longitudinal Survey of Youth (NLSY). Despite the overall declines in the incidence of piece rates and commissions, both are increasingly common within finance, insurance, and real estate. The observed growth in performance pay is being led by the broadly defined financial services industries.

We now turn to the incidence of the non-production bonuses (NPBs). These are collected as an additional portion of the National Compensation Survey. The definition of an NPB is "a payment to employees that is not directly related by formula to individual employee productivity." Again, these represent virtually any other type of payment that is not straight time rates or that does not meet the BLS definition of incentive pay. We will eventually break these down more explicitly to give a flavor of their variety, but two important points must be understood in observing their incidence. First, it is crucial to recognize that only some of the types of payments aggregated into the incidence of NPBs are related to performance and should be considered within the original taxonomy presented in Figure A. Many types of NPBs simply represent forms of compensation not tied to performance and so not performance pay.

Second, the methodology for determining the incidence of NPBs should more appropriately be identified as an "access" or "accessibility" measure and *should not be considered a true incidence at all*. To take an example, if one worker in a large plant is identified as the outstanding worker of the month and awarded a cash prize, all the workers eligible (potentially all the workers in the plant) will be listed as having this non-production bonus available and become part of the share of workers "covered" by this particular non-production bonus (Pfuntner 2004). Yet, the methodological issue is broader than this example. While every worker had a chance at winning the employee-of-the-month award, that may not be true for other types of bonuses. Nonetheless, whenever one or more workers within a particular occupational cell surveyed have been provided a particular type of bonus, or a particular type of bonus can be given, all workers are listed as having it accessible. Thus, every observation becomes either a one (someone in the cell has the benefit) or a zero (no one in the cell has the benefit). These are then aggregated with the appropriate employment rates. Thus, even identifying the NPB measure as one of accessibility may be too broad. Perhaps more accurately it might be the share of workers who work in an establishment in which someone within their occupation has access to a bonus. Thus, the measure would seem to yield far larger coverage figures than would other, narrower measures of bonuses.[5]

As a result, the coverage for NPBs shown in the first column of **Table 3** is extremely large. It indicates that the share of workers covered has increased 8.21 percentage points and currently stands at 49.06%, virtually half of all private industry workers. Again, the pattern of growth across occupational groups remains uneven. In what will become a familiar pattern, among the occupations with the largest growth are the managerial and finance professions with a 13 percentage-point increase. The only larger growth rate is that of 16 percentage points in "other professionals." At the same time many of the occupations had growth rates of only a few percentage points (as low as 2 percentage points in installation and repair). Thus, the growth has been very uneven, but the coverage shares are all remarkably high.

TABLE 3 BLS data on coverage of non-production bonuses for private industry workers

	Total	Other profess-ionals	Mgmt.	Sales	Clerical	Service	Con-struct/ Primary	Install, maintain repair	Prod-uction	Trans-port
1995-96	40.85%	38.35%	50.85%	36.75%	45.34%	27.00%	41.19%	50.30%	50.79%	43.69%
1997-98	40.80	37.68	46.83	38.21	44.61	28.39	42.85	49.46	50.73	42.89
1999-2000	44.30	43.18	51.48	40.25	41.80	30.73	49.19	54.41	54.29	43.84
2001-02	49.29	53.19	58.79	41.19	53.71	37.66	53.38	56.30	55.52	45.80
2003-04	49.35	54.23	62.60	41.19	55.21	35.96	51.01	53.88	54.89	47.31
2005-06	49.06	54.76	63.48	41.81	55.59	35.19	46.80	52.29	55.80	47.70

Note: These are aggregated from quarterly data provided by a special tabulation from the Bureau of Labor Statistics. Each number represents the percentage of workers in the particular industry in jobs where non-production bonuses are paid. Non-production bonuses are distinct from the types of individual performance pay covered in Table 2, which excluded most bonuses, employee of the year awards and, indeed, any payments at the discretion of the employer (whether tied to performance or not). Table 5 describes the specific types of bonuses that make up non-production bonuses.

Source: Authors' calculations from Bureau of Labor Statistics data.

We now try to better understand the high coverage shares for the non-production bonuses. **Table 4** reproduces the detail from the National Compensation Survey used to build up the non-production bonus coverage rates. The figures are from 2006 and the coverage rate that year is 46% (reflecting both a slight decline in 2006 and the difference from the quarterly average technique in Table 3). This figure comes from the aggregation of the individual types of bonuses that are being investigated. Those specific types are listed in the column with their percentages rounded to the nearest whole percent. The sum of the individual types exceeds the 46% as more than one type of bonus can be offered simultaneously.

The individual coverage by type of bonus in Table 4 shows that for many types of bonuses the coverage is only a percentage point or two. More importantly, the bonus types often seem unrelated to performance on the job. Thus, a hiring bonus is a one-time payment given to a new employee at the time of hiring. Such a signing bonus may reflect ability and performance on past jobs but should not be identified as performance pay on the current job. Holiday bonuses are usually small and identical across workers.

TABLE 4 A breakdown by type of non-production bonus (March 2006)

	Coverage	Clearly related to performance	Unlikely to be part of a tournament	Likely to be wide in scope
Total NPB	46%			
Attendance bonus	2	*	*	
Cash profit sharing bonus	5	*	*	*
Employee recognition bonus	4	*		
End of year bonus	11	*	*	*
Holiday bonus	10		*	*
In lieu of benefits bonus	4		*	*
Safety bonus	1	*	*	
Suggestion bonus	2	*	*	
Hiring bonus	2		*	
Longevity bonus	1		*	
Referral bonus	7	*	*	
Retention bonus	1		*	
Union related bonus	1		*	*
Management incentive bonus	1			
Other bonus	6		*	*

Source: Table 26, pp. 31 – 32 of *Employee Compensation Survey: Benefits in Private Industry in the United States- March 2006*, US Department of Labor, Bureau of Labor Statistics, August 2006.

Similarly, in lieu of benefits bonuses should not be identified as performance pay. These are cash payments that take the place of in-kind fringe benefits that would typically be provided, such as health insurance or a retirement plan. **Table 5** provides the exact definitions of most of the types of bonuses.

TABLE 5 Key definitions for non-production bonuses

Attendance bonus – A payment to employees who achieve a specified attendance goal. For example, all employees that take two days of sick leave or fewer within a given year are paid an attendance bonus of $500.

Cash profit sharing – Payment to employees in recognition of their contribution to company profitability. Payments may vary by length of service.

Employee recognition bonus – A payment to employees that rewards performance or significant accomplishments, such as an employee-of-the-month award.

End-of-year bonus – A payment to employees near the end of the year as a sign of appreciation for working hard throughout the year.

Holiday bonus – A payment to employees at a holiday as a sign of appreciation. This payment is usually a token payment with all employees receiving the same amount.

Payment in lieu of benefits – A payment to employees in lieu of the employer providing a benefit such as heath care. In some cases, the employer offers cash to employees who waive employer-sponsored benefits, such as sick leave.

Safety bonus – A payment to employees for maintaining a high level of safety in the workplace. For example, a department receives a bonus for experiencing no injury days during a quarter.

Suggestion bonus – A payment to employees whose innovative suggestions to create better work processes and improve establishment efficiency have been considered or implemented.

Hiring bonus – A payment made by an employer to induce an individual to accept employment with the company.

Referral bonus – A payment given to employees for recommending a qualified applicant who is hired by the establishment.

Longevity bonus – A bonus or a lump-sum payment of some kind (for example, a government savings bond or add-on to severance pay) paid to employees based upon their length of service.

Other bonus – A payment to employees not applicable to other listed non-production bonus categories. Examples include birthday bonuses and retirement bonuses.

Source: "Technical Note," pp. 33 – 34 of *Employee Compensation Survey: Benefits in Private Industry in the United States- March 2006*, U.S. Department of Labor, Bureau of Labor Statistics, August 2006.

As mentioned earlier, some bonuses are better thought of as tournaments in which one or only a few workers actually receive them (employee-of-the-month, for example). These bonuses are likely to have far lower incidence than the coverage variables indicate. Still other bonuses are open to everyone but very few will be able to actually receive them. These might include bonuses for suggestions, referrals, and attendance. In the three final columns of Table 4 we have tried to indicate which benefits we feel reasonably confident are tied to performance, not tournaments, and widely available. As indicated, it represents only a small fraction of the total coverage indicated. In the end, the access coverage figures that emerge for profit sharing and end-of-year bonuses do not seem at odds with those from the more representative micro-data sets we examine later and suggest only a modest incidence of bonuses clearly related to performance and routinely paid to workers.[6]

An important note remains worthy of emphasis before finishing this discussion of the BLS surveys. The NPBs do not represent a large employer cost. While recognizing that much of what are classified as NPBs is not performance pay, we are able to identify the broad costs associated with the NPBs. Specifically, in the first year in which data were published, 1986, they represented 0.7% of hourly compensation. This figure rose to 1.5% of total compensation or $.33 per employee hour worked by March 2003. In a common pattern, the average represented $0.53 per hour for white-collar workers, $0.17 per hour for blue-collar workers, and only $0.06 per hour for service workers. Thus, NPBs as a share of compensation remain very low although increasing. Again, even this share exaggerates the share of compensation comprised by NPBs that are performance pay. These numbers are all taken from Pfuntner (2004, 12).

Again, many things identified as bonuses in the BLS survey are not performance pay. Bonuses given in lieu of a pay raise or employer-provided health insurance do not represent an innovation designed to increase productivity or profit. Instead, they represent reduced compensation in the future and might be better thought of as simply reducing labor costs.

A brief look at the Panel Study of Income Dynamics

The Panel Study of Income Dynamics (PSID) provides a representative sample of the workforce for an unusually long period. Yet, as Lemieux et al. (2007) say, the "constructed measures of performance pay are relatively crude." For the years 1976 to 1992 workers were asked the amount of money they received from bonus, commissions, or overtime. Using other questions, the overtime workers can be excluded. In addition, workers not exclusively paid by time rates are asked how they are paid: piece rates, commission, etc. In later years the workers are asked more directly about the amounts earned by bonuses and commissions. Placing all categories of variable pay into a single category, Lemieux et al. (2007) can develop two types of time series for a sample of male heads of households employed in the private sector. The first measures the simple incidence of reporting performance pay in a given year. By this measure the incidence moves from about 12% of all workers in 1976 and increases to around 16% by 1998. In this time series most of the growth happens in the 1980s, and the incidence in the early 1990s exceeds slightly that of the late 1990s (see Figure 2a of Lemieux et al. 2007). The second measure identifies a job as a performance pay job if the worker ever receives performance pay. Thus, even though the worker may not be reporting performance pay in a particular year, they have reported in the past or will report in the future for their current job. As expected, this dramatically increases the incidence and the resulting series shows more growth: from a little more than 30% in the late 1970s to more than 40% in the 1990s. The overall mean incidence for the panel is 37%.

This second measure seems high given what we know about the churning of performance pay plans from other countries. Establishment surveys in both Germany (Jirjahn 2002) and Australia (Brown and Heywood 2003) indicate that across years firms adopt and drop particular types of performance pay with some regularity.[7] This experimentation in payment methods makes it likely that some of the PSID workers who once report and then fail to report performance pay are reflecting changes in firm policies.[8] Even when this is not true, performance pay schemes that make a payment only one year out of several would tend to be viewed as rather low-powered incentive devices.

Table 6 compares the beginning and end of the time series and uses the annual incidence for actually receiving three types of performance pay after implementing the survey weights. The incidences are based on relatively modest annual sample sizes of around a thousand prime-age male workers. Table 6 shows an extremely low incidence of piece rates, less than 1% of the male sample, and even that seems to be declining slightly. It shows a larger incidence of commissions between 3% and 4%, but it is also declining. The largest category—and the one that is growing—is bonuses. The incidence increased from 9.7% to about 11.0% of all workers.

The PSID averages do not suggest a huge change in the incidence of performance pay. Recognizing that the growth in the incidence of performance pay jobs is greater, it is possible that there is a large increase in jobs that use some performance pay but use it only periodically (less than annually). Moreover, within the general pattern of an increasing use of performance pay, the use of bonuses (for which performance measurement is more likely to be judgmental) has increased, while use of the more formulaic commissions

---

TABLE 6 Incidence of performance pay in the PSID

	1976		1998	
Bonuses	9.749%	(n= 895)	10.970%	(n=933)
Commissions	3.972%	(n=1290)	3.254%	(n=1005)
Piece rates	0.939%	(n=1290)	0.935%	(n=1005)

Note: The sample consists of male heads of household aged 18 to 65 as assembled by Lemiuex et al. (2006). Thanks are expressed to Daniel Parent for providing the reported incidences.

and piece rates has decreased. Finally, we emphasize that within the growing category of bonuses, the PSID does not explicitly require that these be bonuses tied to a measure of performance. This raises the possibility that what is being observed is, in part, an increase in variable pay rather than performance pay.

A more detailed look at the National Longitudinal Survey

This next section looks at data drawn from the National Longitudinal Survey of Youth (NLSY79). The NLSY has the advantage of a larger sample size and more detailed questions on performance pay. It has the disadvantage of not asking the questions on performance pay in every wave and of following a single cohort (respondents of age 14-22 in 1979). The critical questions on performance pay are asked for three years at the end of the 1980s (1988, 1989, and 1990) and then again for three years approximately a decade latter (1996, 1998, and 2000). Thus, we can, at minimum, track the use of performance pay among this cohort over approximately a decade, a time in which the use of performance pay has been thought to increase. We examine what types of performance pay are observed for a nationally representative cohort that entered the labor market in the early 1980s.

We limit our sample to private-sector workers who are employed more than 20 hours per week. We use the cross-sectional weights and initially simply examine the share of workers within a year who identify themselves as receiving particular forms of performance pay. We trim the data slightly to eliminate workers who report earnings below $1.00 per hour and above $100.00 per hour (this restriction does not affect the pattern of results).

We examine two broad questions. The first asks whether or not each respondent receives individual performance pay and if they answer yes, they are asked which of the following they receive: piece rates, commissions, tips, bonuses, or stock options. The second question asks if the respondents receive profit sharing as part of their compensation. Thus, we examine five forms of individual performance pay that all represent variable pay (not built into the base) and one form of group pay also not part of the base and which may or may not be designated for retirement portfolios.

As each year has a relatively limited number of observations in some of the categories of performance pay, we also aggregate the three early years and the three later years. The incidence measures represent the share of annual worker observations over the three years that report receiving the particular type of performance pay. We recognize that a very large share of the workers are identical across years but feel that this aggregation allows a more precise estimate and note that it remains essentially a weighted average of the incidence figures from the three years.[9]

The first panel of **Table 7** presents the incidence figures for individual performance pay showing that approximately one-quarter of workers report at least one form of individual performance pay. There is a very modest increase in the incidence over the decade. The aggregate of the three early years shows an incidence of approximately

TABLE 7 Proportion of workers receiving performance pay (in the NLSY79)

Individual performance pay	1988	1989	1990	1988-90	1996	1998	2000	1996-2000
Any	24.82%	25.98%	26.87%	25.88%	28.46%	27.90%	28.15%	28.17%
Piece rate	2.78%	2.54%	3.02%	2.78%	2.20%	2.30%	1.93%	2.14%
Commission	6.44%	6.67%	7.30%	6.80%	5.81%	5.33%	5.16%	5.43%
Tips	3.81%	3.92%	3.53%	3.76%	2.75%	2.21%	20.00%	2.32%
Bonus	13.87%	14.66%	15.65%	14.71%	15.96%	17.17%	17.69%	16.94%
Stock options	1.09%	1.23%	1.32%	1.21%	3.09%	4.66%	5.64%	4.46%
Sample size	6,834	6,756	6,647	20,237	5,311	5,182	4,974	15,467
Profit sharing	31.64%	33.33%	34.06%	33.01%	32.25%	32.09%	31.93%	32.09%
Sample size	6,434	6,579	6,495	19,508	5,183	5,082	4,866	15,131

Note: The sample consists of private-sector, non-self-employed workers with greater than 20 normal weekly hours. It excludes workers with less than $1 and greater than $100 in hourly wages. All proportions are weighted using NLSY cross-sectional sampling weights. Cells in the row labeled "Any" contain the percentage of respondents receiving piece rates, commissions, tips, bonuses, or stock options in the given year. The rows that follow report the percentage receiving these various types of performance pay. These are not mutually exclusive categories. Profit sharing percentages are obtained from a separate question and considered apart from individual per formance pay. The 1988-1990 column reports the aggregated percentages for the years 1988, 1989, and 1990. The 1996-2000 column reports the aggregated percentages for 1996, 1998, and 2000. We recognize that a very large share of the workers are identical across years but feel that this aggregation allows a more precise estimate and note that it remains essentially a weighted average of the incidence figures from the three years.

Source: Authors' calculations. See Note.

26% and the aggregation of the later years shows an incidence of approximately 28%. The modest increase hides more dramatic patterns by type of performance pay.

The incidence of piece rates is low, only 2.0% or 3.0%, but shows a reasonably large percentage decline. Thus, in the early years the incidence is 2.8%, but it falls to 2.1% by the later years. This decline is matched by a decline in the use of commissions. In the early years 6.8% of workers report commissions, while in the later years only 5.4% report receiving commissions. Equally dramatic, there has been a large percentage decline (admittedly upon a small base) in the share of workers who report receiving a share of their earnings in tips. In the early years, the average incidence is 3.8%, but by the later years this has fallen to 2.3%. Thus, a relatively firm conclusion from the NLSY data is that the share of workers who earn individual performance pay tied by formula to output has fallen over this time period. Indeed, one can sum the share of workers receiving the first three categories of output pay (not exactly correct as some workers may receive more than one of the three forms) and see that in the early years fully 13.3% of workers fell into one of these categories but that by the later years only 9.9% of workers fell into these categories.

This trend in the NLSY might be considered unique to following a single cohort. As workers age a decade, they may be less likely to be in jobs tying earnings to formulaic measures of output. While there may be some truth to this, we emphasize that the PSID—a smaller but representative sample—also showed a decline in the incidence of piece rates and commissions. Such declines continue a many decades long pattern within the United States with Carlson (1982) identifying a secular decline in the use of formulaic based pay over the post-war period up to 1980.

Yet, the overall pattern shows an increase in the incidence of individual performance pay over the years covered by the NLSY. This comes in two forms. First, the share of workers who receive bonuses tied to performance has risen. In the early years, 14.7% of workers reported receiving individual bonuses making it the most common form of individual performance pay. By the later years, 16.9% of workers reported receiving bonuses. The data provide no indication how these bonuses are tied to performance. They may be end-of-year bonuses based on attendance or achievement of specific targets, but they are likely to be largely comprised of bonuses dependent upon a supervisory appraisal (Geddes and Heywood 2003) and may be properly classified as largely judgmental.

Finally, stock options, often reserved for upper managerial personnel, have increased the most dramatically of any category in both percentage and absolute terms. In the early years of the NLSY only 1.2% of workers reported such options, but by the later years this figure increased to 4.5%. This figure seems particularly likely to reflect that we are following a particular cohort. As the cohort ages into their prime earning years, they are more likely to be in positions that provide stock options.

The NLSY also asks respondents an independent question regarding whether or not they receive profit sharing. This is obviously a group form of performance pay and is variable. What we cannot tell is the extent to which this profit sharing represents a form of retirement earnings that cannot be easily accessed until late in life or simply compensation available at the end of each year. The results on the incidence of profit sharing are reported in the second panel of Table 7. Interestingly, the share of the workers reporting profit sharing has been relatively constant decreasing only modestly from 33.0% of private-sector workers to 32.1% of private-sector workers.

We take three general points from these basic figures from the NLSY. First, two of the identified forms of performance pay, profit sharing and stock options, have no public sector equivalent. Second, the formulaic forms of individual performance pay continue to decline in importance as they have for many years prior to this snapshot. Third, the growth in performance pay is concentrated among bonus payments. These payments are often the result of a supervisory appraisal, and their growth has been significant but not overwhelming. In total, an additional 2.2% of workers report receiving bonuses compared to a decade earlier.

To provide further detail on the movements within the use of performance pay in the NLSY we broke out the incidence of pay type by union status and by gender. These results are shown in **Table 8**. As might be anticipated, individual performance pay is less common among union members, and the aggregate evidence suggests the divergence is growing. By the later time period the incidence of performance pay in the non-union sector grew to virtually double that in the union sector (29.9% vs. 15.8%). Importantly, both the union and the non-union sector saw declines in all of the most formulaic individual performance pay—piece rates, commissions, and tips. The growing divergence is being exclusively driven by the changing pattern of bonus payments. Within the non-union sector, the incidence of bonuses increased from roughly 15% to 18%, while within the union sector bonuses fell from 10% to 8%. Thus, the rise in performance pay is limited to bonuses in the non-union sector

The difference by gender shown in Table 8 provides an equally stark portrait. First, there is a very large increase in the use of individual performance pay for men with the aggregate incidence increasing nearly 5 percentage points and almost reaching one-third of all men by the later period. Among women the incidence remains far lower, around 23%, and actually *falls* over the period. These gender differences deserve more scrutiny. For the three types of formulaic performance pay, piece rates, commissions, and tips, the incidence falls for both men and women although more dramatically for women. The real difference that emerges is in the incidence of bonuses. First, men are

TABLE 8 Performance pay by union status and sex (in the NLSY79)

Individual performance pay	Non-union		Union		Male		Female	
	1980s	*1990s*	*1980s*	*1990s*	*1980s*	*1990s*	*1980s*	*1990s*
Any	26.97%	29.89%	18.48%	15.82%	27.65%	32.18%	23.70%	23.28%
Piece rate	2.48%	2.04%	4.82%	2.90%	2.91%	2.42%	2.62%	1.81%
Commission	7.48%	6.01%	2.20%	1.29%	8.16%	6.95%	5.13%	3.58%
Tips	4.07%	2.54%	1.65%	0.78%	2.51%	1.46%	5.29%	3.37%
Bonus	15.32%	18.18%	10.63%	8.06%	16.73%	20.06%	12.25%	13.12%
Stock options	1.24%	4.73%	1.00%	2.54%	1.56%	5.61%	0.79%	3.05%
Sample size	17,481	13,661	2,819	1,806	10,947	8,320	9,920	7,147
Profit sharing	33.27%	32.70%	31.28%	27.72%	33.38%	32.26%	32.56%	31.88%
Sample size	16,805	13,354	2,703	1,777	10,624	8,160	8,884	6,971

Note: The sample consists of private-sector, non-self-employed workers with greater than 20 normal weekly hours. It excludes workers with less than $1 and greater than $100 in hourly wages. All proportions are weighted using NLSY cross-sectional sampling weights. Cells in the row labeled "Any" contain the percentage of respondents receiving piece rates, commissions, tips, bonuses, or stock options. The rows that follow report the percentage receiving these various types of performance pay. These are not mutually exclusive categories. Profit sharing percentages are obtained from a separate question and considered apart from individual performance pay. The 1980s columns report the aggregated percentages for 1988, 1989, and 1990. The 1990s columns report the aggregated percentages for 1996, 1998, and 2000. We recognize that a very large share of the workers are identical across years but feel that this aggregation allows a more precise estimate and note that it remains essentially a weighted average of the incidence figures from the three years.

Source: Authors' calculations. See Note.

TABLE 9 Performance pay by industry (in the NLSY79)

Individual performance pay	Agriculture, mining, and construction		Manufacturing		Transportation, communication, and utilities		Wholesale and retail trade		Finance and real estate		Business and personal services		Professional and related services	
	1980s	1990s	1980s	1990s	1980s	1990s	1980s	1990s	1980s	1990s	1980s	1990s	1980s	1990s
Any	18.02%	21.08%	23.14%	26.44%	26.14%	29.82%	35.67%	33.57%	30.60%	43.73%	32.15%	35.63%	13.78%	15.98%
Piece rate	4.58%	02.82%	5.57%	3.08%	2.47%	2.69%	1.93%	1.87%	0.80%	0.94%	2.05%	2.97%	0.36%	0.53%
Commission	2.60%	03.21%	4.30%	2.55%	7.69%	4.99%	10.47%	8.54%	11.69%	13.47%	11.75%	9.77%	1.22%	0.92%
Tips	0.36%	00.39%	0.29%	0.10%	2.00%	0.47%	10.85%	7.62%	0.70%	0.28%	8.17%	5.82%	0.05%	0.12%
Bonus	11.68%	12.46%	13.77%	18.03%	13.49%	19.46%	16.62%	16.67%	21.02%	28.46%	15.80%	18.34%	11.83%	11.09%
Stock options	0.45%	01.38%	1.81%	5.33%	1.66%	7.85%	1.89%	4.08%	0.59%	8.54%	0.98%	4.99%	0.23%	1.81%
Sample size	2,180	1,530	4,857	3,528	1,347	1,352	4,651	2,858	1,501	1,074	2,676	2,043	3,004	2,845
Profit sharing	18.06%	17.56%	43.65%	44.43%	39.13%	37.83%	33.78%	34.82%	48.83%	42.33%	23.74%	22.61%	22.84%	21.07%
Sample size	2,119	1,479	4,678	3,468	1,307	1,329	4,480	2,808	1,442	1,060	2,578	1,961	2,887	2,796

Note: The sample consists of private-sector, non-self-employed workers with greater than 20 normal weekly hours. It excludes workers with less than $1 and greater than $100 in hourly wages. All proportions are weighted using NLSY cross-sectional sampling weights. Cells in the row labeled "Any" contain the percentage of respondents receiving piece rates, commissions, tips, bonuses, or stock options. The rows that follow report the percentage receiving these various types of performance pay. These are not mutually exclusive categories. Profit sharing percentages are obtained from a separate question and considered apart from individual performance pay. The 1980s columns report the aggregated percentages for 1988, 1989, and 1990. The 1990s columns report the aggregated percentages for 1996, 1998, and 2000. We recognize that a very large share of the workers are identical across years but feel that this aggregation allows a more precise estimate and note that it remains essentially a weighted average of the incidence figures from the three years.

Source: Authors' calculations. See Note.

significantly more likely to receive bonuses than are women.[10] More critically, women experience only a very modest growth in bonuses, not enough to outweigh the decline in other forms of individual performance pay. It increases from 12.3% to 13.1%. This is far smaller than the increase in the incidence for men, from 16.7% to over 20%. The lessons from Table 7 and 8 are then at least two-fold. First, the increase in performance pay is driven almost entirely by the increases in bonuses, and that other measures are generally declining. Second, this critical increase in bonuses remains concentrated almost entirely among non-union males.[11]

To provide yet more detail to this picture, we break the NLSY data down by major industry groups as shown in **Table 9**. The evidence is telling as both the industry group with the greatest use of the aggregate measure of individual performance pay and the industry group with the largest increase in individual performance pay is finance, insurance, and real estate. The share of workers receiving individual performance pay grew from 31% to 44%. All of the other industrial groups show increases of a couple of percentage points, and in the case of wholesale and retail trade, a decline of a couple of percentage points. Interestingly, the use of commissions fell in every industry group except finance, insurance, and real estate in which it increased. Stock options showed an eight-fold increase in use in this same industrial group. In short, it sharply stands out as the industrial group with the most dramatic increases and represents a finding confirmed by both the BLS and NLSY data.

Table 10 breaks down the figures by major occupational groupings. This provides yet more rich grist for the mill. Traditional occupations with high use of individual performance pay such as sales have shown huge declines from 61% to 44% in the aggregate measure. Indeed, the result is driven by the fact that a far smaller share of sales workers receives commissions. The overall incidence of individual performance pay also falls among all service workers and also among operatives and laborers. It increases less than one percentage point among farmers and farm workers. The incidence increases two percentage points among clerical and administrative workers driven by an increase in stock options and despite a decline in bonuses. The incidence among manufacturing and technical workers increases 4 percentage points divided between increases in bonuses and stock options. Finally, incidence among managerial and professional workers increases from 27% to 34%. This 7 percentage-point increase comes from very large increases in the incidence of stock options combined with even larger increases in the incidence of bonuses.

The overall pattern from the NLSY is one that shows a modest increase in individual performance pay that is spread very unevenly across types of performance pay, types of workers, and industries. Output-based formulaic performance pay (piece rates, commissions, and tips) has generally declined while bonuses have been rapidly expanded. This expansion is largely a non-union, male phenomenon concentrated among managers and professionals and in finance, insurance, and real estate. Indeed, the growth is sufficiently uneven that despite the general increase in individual performance pay, it has declined modestly for women, for entire industrial groups, and for entire occupational groups.

TABLE 10 Performance pay by occupation (in the NLSY79)

Individual performance pay	Professional, technical, and kindred		Sales		Clerical and administrative support		Precision production and craftsman		Operatives and laborers		Farmers and farm laborers		Service	
	1980s	*1990s*	*1980s*	*1990s*	*1980s*	*1990s*	*1980s*	*1990s*	*1980s*	*1990s*	*1980s*	*1990s*	*1980s*	*1990s*
Any	27.14%	33.92%	60.73%	43.89%	15.59%	17.60%	19.15%	23.23%	23.97%	20.27%	23.33%	24.34%	33.75%	29.96%
Piece rate	0.54%	0.48%	1.55%	0.95%	0.99%	1.07%	4.41%	4.87%	7.68%	5.02%	5.44%	5.72%	1.31%	0.94%
Commission	6.81%	4.02%	46.03%	26.01%	2.13%	2.18%	4.33%	3.81%	3.23%	1.95%	...	...	4.80%	3.83%
Tips	1.06%	0.62%	0.71%	0.86%	0.63%	0.17%	0.21%	0.23%	2.23%	1.20%	2.25%	1.12%	24.12%	17.39%
Bonus	20.75%	26.15%	29.57%	22.10%	12.20%	11.52%	10.95%	12.41%	10.92%	10.11%	15.64%	13.02%	7.26%	7.80%
Stock options	2.30%	7.71%	1.68%	5.99%	0.51%	1.08%	0.81%	2.04%	0.87%	2.07%	...	...	0.60%	1.74%
Sample size	4,872	4,431	986	1,426	3,994	2,186	2,534	1,960	4,840	3,273	214	259	2,777	1,852
Profit sharing	39.25%	34.87%	42.53%	41.08%	39.99%	36.73%	27.57%	25.62%	29.24%	31.66%	15.13%	18.03%	14.97%	18.84%
Sample size	4,725	4,392	953	1,402	3,836	2,137	2,462	1,930	4,646	3,153	210	244	2,661	1,795

Note: The sample consists of private-sector, non-self-employed workers with greater than 20 normal weekly hours. It excludes workers with less than $1 and greater than $100 in hourly wages. All proportions are weighted using NLSY cross-sectional sampling weights. Cells in the row labeled "Any" contain the percentage of respondents receiving piece rates, commissions, tips, bonuses, or stock options. The rows that follow report the percentage receiving these various types of performance pay. These are not mutually exclusive categories. Profit sharing percentages are obtained from a separate question and considered apart from individual performance pay. The 1980s columns report the aggregated percentages for 1988, 1989, and 1990. The 1990s columns report the aggregated percentages for 1996, 1998, and 2000. We recognize that a very large share of the workers are identical across years but feel that this aggregation allows a more precise estimate and note that it remains essentially a weighted average of the incidence figures from the three years.

Source: Authors' calculations. See Note.

National Study of the Changing Workplace

The National Study of the Changing Workplace (NSCW) is a representative sample of currently employed U.S. workers. Sponsored by the Families and Work Institute, the NSCW provides detailed information on the work lives and family lives of the workforce. The survey is undertaken every five years and has been published in 1993, 1998, and 2003. Broadly based on the Department of Labor's 1977 Quality of Employment Survey, it asks a series of common questions in each wave. In addition, a set of questions unique to each wave is added.

The most recent wave from 2003 asks a unique and broad question on the receipt of performance pay. "At your job are pay increases, bonuses, and promotions directly and clearly related to your performance?" Thus, unlike any of the measures in the previously examined data sources, this question encourages workers to include base pay that may be related to their performance. Thus, if an annual evaluation influences the size of a worker's earnings for the next year, this would be included in the NSCW measure. Beyond that, workers are asked to indicate whether promotions associated with their employment are linked to performance. It also obviously includes types of variable performance pay such as piece rates, tips, and bonuses but would not include variable pay unrelated to performance. Interestingly, the positive responses to the question might exclude those types of performance pay that workers think fail to reward their performance. Therefore, if a scheme is arbitrary or subject to strategic manipulation by supervisors, it is possible that workers could respond that the scheme is *not* "directly and clearly related to your performance." Thus, the NSCW provides a measure that is not only extremely broad in its scope, but also asks implicitly that workers pass at least some judgment upon its success. At minimum, workers would seem to be passing judgment on at least the pay scheme's transparency and connection to performance.

As in several of our earlier examinations, we limit our sample to the private sector, and we also examine those who typically work at least 20 hours per week. This yields a sample of 1,768. Using the sampling weights, the resulting mean of the performance pay variable indicates that approximately 60% of U.S. private-sector workers report that their earnings or promotions are tied to performance. This number is not unusually large given the broad nature of the question and given earlier numbers derived from similarly broad questions. Boyd (1994) in his cross-country examination of attitudes toward work found that 68% of U.S. workers claimed their pay depended on performance. He cautions, however, that the U.S. workers lead the world in the proportion that think their pay *should* depend on performance. Thus, we are careful to recognize that responses to the broad NSCW question potentially involve worker perceptions and projections that may not be accurate. Nonetheless, we have no *a priori* idea how such a potential would bias the estimates we present.

We use positive responses to the performance pay questions as a dependent variable in a probability model of its determinants. We estimate a linear probability model, but note that fitting a cumulative normal (probit) does not greatly alter the pattern of results.

Before moving to those estimations we present the means of the independent variables that will enter the estimations in **Table 11**. These means are presented separately by whether or not the worker responds positively that their pay or promotion is related to performance. The first column presents the means for those responding positively and the second column presents the means for those who do not respond positively. The sample that reports positively that it has performance driven pay is comprised of more women, is younger and better educated. It is disproportionately outside of rural areas but is concentrated in the Midwest. There appears to be no differences in the non-white share.

The job characteristics indicate that only 5.0% of those reporting performance pay are union members while 23.1% of those not reporting performance pay are union members. The average tenure is 6.2 years for those reporting performance pay but a full two years longer for those not reporting performance pay. Those reporting performance pay are concentrated in medium-sized establishments (a small establishment is less than 25 employees, medium is 26 to 500, and large is more than 500) when compared with those not reporting performance pay. Those reporting performance pay earn $3.46 more per hour on average than do those not reporting performance pay. This represents

TABLE 11 Descriptive statistics, 2003 National Study of the Changing Workplace

	Reports pay is related to performance	Reports that pay is not related to performance
Demographics		
Female	46.43%	43.10%
Non-white	20.04	19.85
Age	38.92	42.01
High school educated	64.83	63.57
College educated	26.52	21.51
Rural	19.37	26.06
East	20.02	20.01
Midwest	35.67	31.61
South	28.17	30.38
West	16.15	18.01
Job-related characteristics		
Union	5.08%	23.05%
Tenure	6.20	8.20
Mid-sized establishment	51.10	46.12
Large establishment	16.09	19.01
Hourly earnings	21.27	16.81

Continued on next page

Continued from previous page

TABLE 11 Descriptive statistics, 2003 National Study of the Changing Workplace

	Reports pay is related to performance	Reports that pay is not related to performance
Industry		
Agriculture, mining, and construction	12.81%	10.57%
Manufacturing	13.36	23.26
Transportation	7.30	10.51
Wholesale and retail trade	23.17	20.68
Finance, insurance, and real estate	10.10	2.06
Professional service	31.29	30.88
Private service	1.98	2.04
Occupation		
Executives and management	17.50%	8.54%
Professionals	13.57	15.04
Technical	4.52	4.31
Production and repair	26.31	39.82
Sales	12.81	7.36
Administrative support	15.02	12.20
Service	10.27	12.74
Sample size	1,087	681

Note: Reported are the means or proportions for the subsample receiving performance pay and not receiving performance pay, respectively, in the NSCW. The NSCW is a nationally representative cross-section of workers. A respondent is considered to receive performance pay if he or she affirms that pay increases, bonuses and promotions are "directly and clearly related to your performance." The sample excludes public sector workers, self-employed workers, those working fewer than 20 hours a week, and those whose information is missing for key variables. All proportions are weighted using NSCW sampling weights.

Source: Authors' calculations. See Note.

a 20.6% difference in earnings. The patterns across occupations and industries remain familiar despite the extremely broad and different measure of performance pay. Those reporting performance pay are disproportionately concentrated in executive and managerial jobs and sales jobs. The industry of finance, insurance, and real estate shows one of the largest percentage disparities, representing a bit more than 10.0% of the workers reporting performance pay but only 2.0% of those not reporting performance pay. Those working in primary industries and wholesale and retail trade are also more prominent among the respondents reporting performance pay, while manufacturing comprises a much larger share of the workers not receiving performance pay.

We now turn to the issue of the relative importance of these factors in predicting whether or not respondents report performance pay. The first column of **Table 12** presents a parsimonious specification using demographics and human capital controls. Neither women nor non-whites report performance pay with a significantly different probability. Age, however, plays a very clear role. Older workers are significantly less likely to report receiving performance pay. The pattern of coefficients decreases monotonically from entry-age workers up to those age 65. Given our access in the NSCW to only a single cross-section, two possibilities exist. First, younger workers are more likely to receive performance pay, and this likelihood decreases as they age. Thus, younger workers may be more willing to accept the earnings risk associated with performance pay or may still be in tournaments where future promotions depend on performance. These conditions then change as the workers age. Alternatively, the pattern may reflect vintage effects. Older workers tend to populate types of jobs that have not traditionally had large elements of performance pay (say, certain segments of large-scale manufacturing), but younger workers are more likely to populate jobs that have traditionally had performance pay (say, sales or management). In this view, the age coefficient might be picking up the changing composition of jobs over the last few decades rather than the influence of workers aging.

Performance pay is more likely among both the high school educated and the college educated than among those who have not completed high school. Performance pay is less likely among those in the rural locations. Significant regional differences do not emerge.

We now augment this specification with the job characteristics. As column 2 shows, adding these controls does not alter the pattern of significant determinants isolated in column 1. Yet, all three of the job characteristics emerge as significant determinants.

There exists a general result that those with more tenure are less likely to report receiving performance pay, but as the detailed categories show, there is no significant difference between those with three to six years of tenure when compared with those with less than three years of tenure. The significant differences emerge between those with substantial lengths of tenure and those with less than three years. Additionally, the pattern does not suggest a monotonic relationship. The influence of the longest tenure category (greater than 20 years) is essentially the same as that of the category that is two smaller (six to 10 years). The concentration of those with performance pay among those with the lowest tenure raises interesting possibilities. First, jobs with performance pay may be the first step in career ladders within firms. Workers might, for example, be required to start in sales before moving up within the company. Alternatively, jobs with performance pay have individual output that can be easily measured suggesting that these workers also have skills that are easily transferred and so turnover is large. Distinguishing among these alternatives would require longitudinal data not available in the NSCW.

The role of medium-size establishments emerges with workers in those establishments 6.6 percentage points more likely to report performance pay—recall this is on an average likelihood of about 60%. Those in large establishments have an insignificant difference in the likelihood of reporting performance pay when compared with those in small firms.

The union result is surprisingly large. Past evidence on the relationship between unions and performance pay has been somewhat mixed (Heywood and Jirjahn 2006).

Indeed, in his study of U.S. performance pay, Brown (1990) sometimes found unions a significant negative determinant but sometimes found them an insignificant determinant. This difference depended on the data source and the specification. Yet, there

TABLE 12 Determinants of performance pay (2003 National Study of the Changing Workplace)

	-1	-2	-3	-4
Demographics				
Female	3.25	-0.29	2.40	-0.19
Non-white	-0.11	1.70	2.19	3.43
Age 25-34	-8.81*	-6.46	-9.66**	-10.02**
Age 35-44	-12.61**	-8.26*	-12.34**	-11.99**
Age 45-54	-17.73**	-10.27**	-13.61**	-14.08**
Age 55-64	-25.10**	-17.46**	-21.16**	-20.71**
Age 65 and older	-13.82	-9.81	-11.77	-9.78
High school educated	15.15**	18.34**	15.31**	14.47**
College educated	19.72**	18.86**	10.72	8.66
Rural	-8.78**	-8.31**	-6.72**	-4.82
Midwest	4.76	1.22	1.46	1.84
South	-0.77	-0.59	-0.16	0.88
West	-3.78	-4.69	-5.04	-5.69
Job-related characteristics				
Union		-39.11**	-40.08**	-37.42**
Tenure of 3-5 years		-4.15	-3.28	-3.04
Tenure of 6-10 years		-11.21**	-11.70**	-10.53**
Tenure of 11-20 years		-7.99*	-9.54**	-9.45**
Tenure of greater than 20 years		-11.47**	-14.04**	-11.44**
Mid-sized establishment		6.57**	5.69*	8.19**
Large establishment		2.24	0.49	5.09
Log earnings			10.13**	8.52**
Industry (professional service omitted)				
Agriculture, mining, and construction				14.85**
Transportation				-1.12
Manufacturing				-6.44
Wholesale and retail trade				0.47
Finance, insurance, and real estate				20.10**
Private service				3.87

Continued on next page

Continued from previous page

TABLE 12 Determinants of performance pay (2003 National Study of the Changing Workplace)

	-1	-2	-3	-4
Occupation (professionals omitted)				
Executives and management				12.11**
Technical				7.58
Production and repair				-0.60
Sales				13.34**
Administrative support				6.96
Service				1.42
R-squared	0.04	0.11	0.13	0.16

Note: Each column is a separately run heteroskedasticty-corrected linear probability model using NSCW sampling weights. The sample size in each column is 1,768. Reported are percentage point effects on the likelihood of pay being performance-related. All variables are measured as dummy variables except log earnings. * and ** indicate determinants statistically significant at the .10 level and .05 level, respectively.

Source: Authors' calculations. See Note.

is little doubt using the broad self-reported measure from the NSCW that unionization plays a critical role. Union members are 39.1 percentage points less likely to claim that their compensation depends upon their performance.

We emphasize that unionization is surely measuring both the institutional influence of representation (and collective bargaining) and the types of jobs that tend to be unionized. Certainly, one prominent theory suggests that unions arise in response to circumstances of team production (inter-dependencies among worker productivities) in which employees share workplace public goods such as the speed of the assembly line, temperature, light, and so on (Duncan and Stafford 1980). The union arises, in part, to play a representative function in determining the preferred level of workplace public goods but the consequence of team production is that it is extremely difficult to isolate individual performance (Alchian and Demsetz 1972). Thus, one might anticipate that apart from the influence of the bargaining objectives of unions, the jobs in which they are prevalent may be less suitable for the type of direct connection between earnings and performance that the question identifies[12] Certainly, the fact that manufacturing workers are concentrated among those not receiving performance pay and that the assembly line is the classic example of team production lends some credence to this view.

We next include the measure of hourly earnings as an explanatory variable. We do so recognizing its potential endogeneity. One of the major purposes of performance pay is to elicit additional effort or output that is then rewarded with higher earnings. Yet, from the perspective of our largely descriptive estimates of who has performance pay, the inclusion plays several roles. First, it is well recognized that performance pay also serves to sort workers according to productivity (Lazear 2000). Thus, those workers who are more productive will sort, and be sorted, into jobs that reward that productivity with performance pay. In this respect, higher earnings serve, in part, as an indicator of productivity and should be positively associated with receiving performance pay. Second, there is enormous variation in the types of jobs that cannot be fully captured by our other controls. Earnings can serve to control for some of these differences that might be driving other results. Thus, controlling for earnings helps hold constant the fact that high-ranking executives, financial planners, and others typically both have high earnings and receive performance pay.

The results in column 3 confirm the anticipated partial correlation between earnings and performance pay. A change of one unit in log earnings is associated with a 10 percentage-point increase in the likelihood of reporting performance pay (the standard deviation in log earnings for the sample is .71). Despite the importance of earnings in the estimation, the remaining job characteristics retain at least as strong a role as they did in column 2. The individual characteristics also look broadly similar, but the role of higher education has diminished as a determinant.

Finally, column 4 adds the one-digit controls for both industry and occupation. Several of these controls emerge as significant determinants. Despite the controls already included, those in finance, insurance, and real estate are 20 percentage points more likely to report performance pay. Those in agriculture, mining, and construction are nearly 15 percentage points more likely to report performance pay relative to the base of professional services. These are the only two statistically significant industrial coefficients. Executives and managers are more than 12 percentage points more likely to report performance pay and those in sales are more than 13 percentage points more likely to report performance pay. These are the only two statistically significant occupational controls.

Despite the fact that nearly 60% of the NSCW claimed to have a direct, clear connection between earnings and promotion and their performance, it remains incorrect to suggest that this figure represents a likelihood shared by all workers in the private sector. This point can be illustrated with a simple projection. Imagine a stockbroker and a manufacturing production worker who have identical characteristics other than their industry, occupation, and union status. To examine the difference in their predicted responses we combine the significant coefficients on unionization, the industry finance, insurance, and real estate and the occupation sales. This summation from column 4 yields 70.9 percentage points. The otherwise equal stockbroker is nearly 71 percentage points more likely to report performance pay. Obviously, this is an imperfect estimate as one would anticipate the stockbroker to earn more working to increase the gap and would be likely to differ in other dimensions that might narrow the gap. Nonetheless, it serves to indicate that it would be highly unlikely to find a stockbroker *not* reporting performance pay and highly unlikely to find a unionized production worker actually reporting performance pay.

Thus, even with our extremely broad and self-reported measure of performance pay we continue to conclude that its incidence is not uniform. Instead, it follows patterns established earlier with the much narrower measures of performance pay that were limited to variable pay and taken from NLSY or the BLS establishment data.

Performance Pay as a Share of Compensation

While our inquiry has largely focused on the prevalence of performance pay in the U.S. labor force, it makes sense to ask about the importance of such pay as a share of compensation. Even if performance pay is far from ubiquitous, it may be crucial for the workers who receive it. In this sense, it may be a critical element of compensation even if for a minority share of the labor force.

Investigating this issue is made difficult by the lack of good measures of both total compensation and of the earnings derived from performance pay in many data sources. For example, neither the NLSY79 nor the NSCW used in the previous section provide the necessary data. Similarly, the BLS data on bonuses do not allow computation of the share of compensation derived from the bonuses. Nonetheless, several data sources allow at least a partial answer.

Lemieux et al. (2007) back out a time series of reasonable length on the size of bonuses from the PSID. They also present a shorter series on a broader definition of performance pay. While unable to identify the value of piece rates, they do identify the amount earned by bonuses, tips, and commissions for the period of 1992 to 1998. While the small number of observations suggests that inferring any trend over this time may be questionable, the median share of total earnings attributable to these sources is 3.5% over the period. This median is conditional upon receiving one or more of these sources of performance pay. The distribution is very skewed right with some workers reporting shares over 40%. While this results in a mean several times larger than the median, Lemieux et al. comment that "...performance pay, *per se*, only represents a relatively modest component of total compensation" (Lemieux et al. 2007, 17). They argue that despite this modest share, performance pay may be a proxy for paying earnings more closely tied to the individual than to the job. This may well be so, but as emphasized in our review of the literature, paying people rather than jobs may involve a closer rewarding of productivity and/or it may involve rewarding personal characteristics that are not associated with productivity such as race, gender, or influence activities.

In an attempt to further add to the evidence, we examined the new cohort of the National Longitudinal Survey started in 1997. The obvious problem with this data is that the sample cohort is very young and so not representative of the population at large. By the end of our examination period, the oldest workers were only 26. The advantage of the data is that it asks workers if they receive commissions, tips, bonuses, or incentive pay. The workers respond separately for each type of performance pay. If the workers indicate that they receive one or more types of performance pay, they are asked to identify their usual earnings associated with performance pay. Specifically, the question asks: "About how much income do you usually receive from [tips, commissions, bonuses, incentives, other] in your job with [your employer]?" These amounts can be compared with the workers' estimates of their total earnings in a question that explicitly encourages them to include performance pay in that estimate. The question asks "During [the year], how much income did you receive from wages, salary, commissions, or tips from all jobs, before deductions for taxes or for anything else?" The comparison between the responses to the two questions provides a rough estimate of the share of compensation due to performance pay.

In constructing this estimate we use all years available, 1997-2005, but limit ourselves to employed workers age 18 or over. We recognize this may include college and university students but are hesitant to exclude them given the ages of the respondents. We also recognize that the sample of those working will likely not be representative of the sample working upon completion of education. We take each respondent year as an observation thus pooling the sample across years. We divide the earnings from performance pay by the total earnings for the year to create an initial estimate of share of earnings. We compute this separately for those reporting each of the types of performance pay.

The results are shown in the first row of **Table 13**. We emphasize several points before discussing them. First, the performance pay earnings include those earnings from all types of performance pay. Hence, if a worker earns both tips and a bonus, they appear in both the column for tips and that for bonuses. Moreover, the performance pay earnings that are listed include the sum from both sources. Thus, we do not have an exact measure of the share of earnings from tips but rather the share of earnings from all sources of performance pay for those who report tips. Second, the performance pay measure is specific to the main job. As a consequence, tips earned in a second job are excluded from the measure of performance pay. The first point potentially overestimates the share of tips in compensation, while the second potentially underestimates the share of tips in compensation.

Understanding this, we note that in no case is the average share of earnings comprised by performance pay particularly large. It is largest for those earning commissions at 10.2% and smallest for those earning incentive pay at 2.0%. Unlike the PSID estimates, these are means rather than medians. Thus, despite the difference in data source, cohort, and construction, the same basic point emerges. Performance pay is a relatively small share of total earnings even among that minority that actually receives performance pay. We do note that our distributions are also very skewed right and that standard deviations are large, especially for commissions. The standard deviation for the share of performance pay earned by those receiving commissions was nearly 49%, suggesting that, as a very rough approximation, something around a fifth of workers receiving commissions may earn the majority of their compensation in that form.[13] Those receiving bonuses earn a smaller mean share, 6.1%, and fewer very large shares.

The share of earnings for those receiving tips and incentive payments are even lower, 3.4% and 2.0%.

The incentive payment is a new designation in the NLSY97. In the NLSY79, workers identified piece rates in the otherwise similar question. A separate piece rate question remains in the NLSY97, but the associated earnings are not identified as part of those earned in the performance pay question itemized above. "Incentive pay" appears to be linked to performance and typically to output. According to NLS user services, incentive pay captures extra money or other forms of compensation awarded for reaching or exceeding certain levels of performance, including meeting established sales or production quotas.[14] Thus, while a valuable designation it cannot be matched with the previous question from the NLSY79.

While we cannot fully correct for the two sources of bias we identify earlier, we can make a partial adjustment to correct for the fact that the performance pay earnings are for the primary job and total earnings are for all jobs. The third row in Table 13 presents the share of earnings from performance pay limited to those who hold a single job. For these workers the earnings from their primary job are their earnings for the year. They do not have multiple jobs. As anticipated, the resulting shares are typically higher but not greatly. Many observations are lost as there are a large number of multiple job holders (both simultaneously and over a year) in this young cohort. Indeed, the estimated share earned for those receiving bonuses actually falls when limited to single job holders.

Finally, one could combine, very imperfectly, the two waves of the NLS to give an indication of the overall importance of particular types of performance pay. In the NLSY79 we suggested that around 17% of those prime-age workers received some type of bonus. From the NLSY97 we computed that bonus earners received 6% of their compensation from individual performance pay. Thus, as an especially rough snapshot, as little as 1% of aggregate compensation comes in the form of bonuses (.06 X .17). We recognize this creates many sins of omission, but we make the estimate only to emphasize that a minority of workers receive bonuses, and those bonuses appear to comprise only a small share of compensation for those that receive them.

TABLE 13 Share of total annual earnings from performance pay (NLSY97)

	Tips	Bonuses	Incentive pay	Commissions
Job performance /annual	3.36%	6.05%	1.98%	10.21%
N (year respondent obs.)	1,882	1,532	419	761
Job performance /job	3.70	5.23	2	10.52
N (year respondent obs.)	741	904	215	349

Note: Entries represent the mean share of total earnings comprised by all sources of performance pay for those workers who report receiving the specific type of performance pay listed in the columns at their main job. Starting in the third row, the sample is limited to holders of a single job in the year.

Source: Center for Effective Organizations as reported by Lawler (2003).

Conclusion

While appeals to comparability provide a motivation for examining the pattern of private-sector performance pay, comparability need not be a blind copying of private-sector incidence. Governmental employers may have fundamentally different objectives on the one hand and different abilities to make long-term commitments on the other hand. A frequent contention is that the rise of performance pay in the private sector mirrors a decline in internal labor markets in which job security and pay progression were taken for granted (Lawler 2003; Cannon et al. 2000). Even in major Japanese corporations—famous for their long-term employment relationships—recent pay system changes that emphasize performance pay, *seikashugi,* are associated with a reduction in the workers' expectations of lifetime employment (Tatsumichi and Morishima 2007). Thus, if reliance on profit sharing and individual performance incentives have replaced internal labor markets, this replacement need not be transferred to governmental employers who retain by design longer-term employment relations.

Yet, apart from such broad theoretical concerns, the data presented in this study serve to suggest that the ubiquitous standard of comparability may provide only weak guidance for typical governmental workforces. While the separate measures of performance pay we examined reveal important differences, it remains the case that the incidence was generally far higher for sales workers, executives, and financial workers. In these cases, there exists a clear individual output measure, units sold or dollars of profit or sales. In short, the assumption that profit should be maximized can be easily translated into performance pay. Governments sell relatively little, and the goal of profit maximization is often simply not relevant.

More generally, if governmental work involves substantial team production and multi-dimensional measures of success (examples might include everything from disease research teams to police and fire functions), then suitable individual measures of performance may be completely absent. Even when they can be devised, they may run a very high risk of "rewarding A while hoping for B." This is not to suggest that there exists no place for rewarding performance in the public sector. Instead, it stands as a caution against several potential fallacies. The suggestion that large shares of the private sector workforce have a tight formulaic relationship between earnings and performance is wrong. The evidence from the PSID, the NLSY, and the BLS all suggest that these kind of relationships are rare—recall the BLS estimate of the incidence of incentive pay at only 6%. Moreover, this type of performance pay seems to be fading if anything. Second, while bonus and merit schemes that use variable performance pay have been growing in use, they are not everywhere. They appear to cover only around one worker in seven in a given year, as suggested by the NLSY. Third, while the majority of the private-sector workforce claims their pay or promotion prospects are tied to their performance, the likelihood of such a claim varies dramatically across different parts of the workforce. Fourth, performance pay appears to comprise only a small portion of total compensation even for the minority that receives such pay. These patterns help to provide important background and facts for thinking about issues of performance pay in the public sector.

Endnotes

1. Related to the distinction between objective (formulaic) and subjective (judgmental) is that suggested by Khalil and Lawaree (1995) of input versus output related measurement. While output-based measures will more typically be objective and input-based measures (effort) will more typically be subjective the correspondence is far from perfect.

2. UK evidence also suggests that performance pay is both growing and more common among larger firms within the private sector (Conyon, Peck, and Read 2001).

3. In order to provide continuity for the 1995 to 2006 period, the BLS classified all occupations using codes from the Standard Occupation Classification (SOC) system. According to the BLS, it was not possible to accurately classify occupations in the ECI by the SOC codes prior to 1995.

4. See Belman et al. (2005) for detail on the use of incentive pay (typically arranged as earnings per mile driven) among over the road truck drivers.

5. Pfuntner (2004, 11) presents his own example to explain the difference between access and coverage. "For example, if an employee in the selected job of chemist worked in an establishment that granted a bonus to chemists with perfect attendance for the year, the employee would be counted as having access to an attendance bonus, regardless if he or she achieved perfect attendance and received such a bonus in the latest year."

6. It should be noted that the BLS was asked for, but was not able to provide, reliable breakdowns on the individual types of bonuses for the time series we examined for the broader aggregation of NPB.

7. Specifically, 26% of establishments in the Australian firm panel either adopted or dropped individual performance pay schemes between 1990 and 1995 (Brown and Heywood 2003).

Similarly, Jirjahn (2002) shows that despite a constant incidence of piece rates among manufacturing firms of 14.6% in 1994 and 1996, the majority of those 14.6% of firms did not have piece rates in both years.

8. The churning observed in the private sector might well be present in the public sector as well considering the need for periodic legislative or other review and the presence of severe cyclical budget constraints for many governments.

9. Indeed, to double check we calculated the average incidence across the three years for the first entry recovering an estimate that differed by only .0001.

10. This is confirmed at the 5% level of significance for both years.

11. We note that the gender differences in incidence may reflect the fact that a disproportionate share of the women work part time. While all workers in our sample work more than 20 hours a week, there may be variation between those that work more or less within this restriction. If part-time status is heavily associated with some types of performance pay, what looks like a gender difference may be misleading.

12. Indeed, European evidence suggests that unions are increasingly amenable to performance pay providing that it is transparent, fair, and easily verifiable (see Van het Karr and Gruenell 2001)

13. This rough approximation follows from recognizing that 16% of a normal distribution lies one standard deviation above its mean and that one standard deviation above the mean would be a share of 59%. We recognize the distribution is not normal but are simply trying to emphasize the great importance of commissions for a relatively small number of those receiving them.

14. The authors thank Steve McClaskie at NLS User Services for this information.

Bibliography

Adams, Christopher. 2006. Optimal team incentives with CES production. *Economics Letters*. Vol. 9, pp. 143–48.

Alchian, Armen, and Harold Demsetz. 1972. Production costs, information, and economic organization. *American Economic Review*. Vol. 62, pp. 777–95.

Antonioni, David. 1996. Designing an effective 360 degree appraisal feedback process. *Organizational Dynamics*. Vol. 25, pp. 24–38.

Asch, Beth J. 1990. Do incentives matter? The case of Navy recruiters. *Industrial and Labor Relations Review*. Vol. 43, pp. S89–106.

Azfar, O., and S. Danninger. 2001.Profit sharing, employment stability, and wage growth. *Industrial and Labor Relations Review*. Vol. 54, pp. 619–30.

Baker, George. 1992. Incentive contracts and performance measurement. *Journal of Political Economy*. Vol. 100, pp. 598–614.

Baker, George, Michael Jensen, and Kevin J. Murphy. 1988. Compensation and incentives: practice vs. theory. *Journal of Finance*. Vol. 18, pp. 593–616.

Ballou, Dale. 2001. Pay for performance in public and private schools. *Economics of Education Review*. Vol. 20, pp. 51–61.

Barkume, Anthony. 2004. Using incentive pay and providing pay supplements in U.S. job markets. *Industrial Relations*. Vol. 43, pp. 618–33.

Barkume, Anthony, and Thomas G. Moehrle. 2004. "Development of an ECI excluding workers earning incentive pay." Bureau of Labor Statistics Working Paper. (prepared for the Federal Economic Statistics Advisory Committee, January 14, 2004).

Belman, Dale, Kristen A. Monaco, and Taggert J. Brooks. 2005. *Sailors of the Concrete Sea*. East Lansing Michigan: Michigan State University Press.

Belman, Dale, and John S. Heywood. 1996. "The Structure of Compensation in the Public Sector." In *Public Sector Employment in a Time of Transition,* pp. 127–162, D. Belman, M. Gunderson and D. Hyatt, eds. Madison Wisc.: Industrial Relations Research Association.

Black, Boyd. 1994. Labour market incentive structures and employee performance: An international comparison. *British Journal of Industrial Relations*. Vol. 32: pp. 99–111.

Brett, Joan F. and Leanne E. Atwater. 2001. 360 degree feedback: Accuracy, reactions and perceptions of usefulness. *Journal of Applied Psychology*. Vol. 86, pp. 930–42.

Brown, Charles. 1990. Firms' choice of method of pay. *Industrial and Labor Relations Review*. Vol. 43, pp. 165s–82s.

Brown, Michelle, and John S. Heywood. 2005. Performance appraisal systems: Determinants and change. *British Journal of Industrial Relations*. Vol. 43, pp. 659–79.

Brown, Michelle, and John S. Heywood. 2003. The determinants of incentive schemes: Australian panel data. *Australian Bulletin of Labour*. Vol. 29, pp. 218–35.

Burgess, Simon, and Marisa Ratto. 2003. The role of incentives in the public sector: Issues and evidence. *Oxford Review of Economic Policy*. Vol. 19, pp. 285–300.

Cannon, Sandra, Bruce Fallick, Michael Littau, and Raven Saks. 2000. "Has compensation become more flexible?" Working Paper, Federal Reserve Board. April.

Carlson, Norma W. 1982. Time rates tighten their hold on manufacturing. *Monthly Labor Review*. Vol. 105, pp. 15–22.

Casalino, Lawrence, G., Caleb Alexander, Lei Jin, and R. Tamara Konetzka. 2007. General internists' views on pay-for-Pperformance and public reporting of quality scores: A national survey. *Health Affairs*. Vol. 26, pp. 492–99.

Conyon, M., S. Peck, and L. Read. 2001. Performance pay and corporate structure in UK firms. *European Management Journal*. Vol. 19, pp. 73–82.

Cooke, William N. 1994. Employee participation programs, group-based incentives, and company performance: A union-nonunion comparison. *Industrial and Labor Relations Review*. Vol. 47, pp. 594–609.

Cragg, Michael. 1997. Performance incentives in the public sector: Evidence from the Job Training Partnership Act. *Journal of Law Economics and Organization*. Vol. 13, pp. 147–68.

Dixit, Avinash. 2002. Incentive and organizations in the public sector: An interpretative review. *Journal of Human Resources*. Vol. 37, pp. 696–727.

Dixit, Avinash. 1997. Power of incentives in private vs. public organizations. *American Economic Review Papers and Proceedings*. Vol. 87, pp. 278–82.

Drago, Robert, and Gerald T. Garvey. 1998. Incentives for helping on the job: Theory and evidence. *Journal of Labor Economics*. Vol. 16, pp. 1–25.

Duncan, Greg, and Frank Stafford. 1980. Do union members receive compensating wage differentials? *American Economic Review*. Vol. 70, pp. 355–71.

Eberts, Randall, Kevin Hollenbeck, and Joe Stone. 2002. Teacher performance incentives and student outcomes. *Journal of Human Resources*. Vol. 37, pp. 913–27.

Edwards, Mark R., and Ann J. Ewen. 1996. *Providing 360 Degree Feedback: An Approach to Enhancing Individual and Organizational Performance*. Scottsdale, Ariz.: American Compensation Association.

Elvira, Marta, and Michael Graham. 2002. Not just a formality: Pay system formalization and sex-related earnings effects. *Organization Science*. Vol. 13, pp. 601–17.

Elvira, Marta, and Robert Town. 2001. The effects of race and worker productivity on performance evaluations. *Industrial Relations*. Vol. 40, pp. 571–90.

FitzRoy, Felix and Kornelius Kraft. 1987. Cooperation, productivity, and profit sharing. *Quarterly Journal of Economics*. Vol. 85, pp. 23–35.

Freeman, Richard B., and Morris M. Kleiner. 2005. The last American shoe manufacturers: Decreasing productivity and increasing profits in the shift from piece rates to continuous flow production. *Industrial Relations*. Vol. 44, pp. 307–30.

Freeman, Richard B., Douglas Kruse, and Joseph Blasi. 2004. "Monitoring colleagues at work: Profit sharing, employee ownership, broad-based stock options, and workplace performance in the United States." Discussion Paper No. 647. London: Centre for Economic Performance.

Friebel, Guido, and Michael Raith. 2004. Abuse of authority and hierarchical communication. *RAND Journal of Economics*. Vol. 35, pp. 224–44.

Gibbons, R. 1998. Incentives and Careers in Organizations. *Journal of Economic Perspectives*. Vol. 12, pp. 115–32.

Gibbons, Robert. 1987. Piece-rate incentive schemes. *Journal of Labor Economics*. Vol. 5, pp. 413–29.

Hansen, Daniel G. 1997. Worker Performance and Group Incentives: A Case Study. *Industrial and Labor Relations Review*. Vol. 51, pp. 37–53.

Heywood, John S. 2005. "Labor Market Institutions and Productivity: The Case of Performance Pay." In *Vision for the Reform of Labor Relations in Korea*. Korean Institute for Industrial Economics and Trade.

Heywood, John S., Olaf Huebler, and Uwe Jirjahn. 1998. Variable payment schemes and industrial relations: Evidence from Germany. *Kyklos*. Vol. 51, pp. 327–57.

Heywood, John S., and Uwe Jirjahn. 2006. "Performance Pay: Determinants and Consequences." In *Contemporary Issues in Employment Relations*. D. Lewin, ed. Champaign, Ill.: Labor and Employment Relations Association. pp. 149–88.

Heywood, John S., and Patrick L. O'Halloran. 2005. Racial earnings differentials and erformance pay. *Journal of Human Resources*. Vol. 40, pp. 435–52.

Hill, Marvin, and Emily DeLacenserie. 1991. Interest criteria in fact-finding and arbitration. *Marquette Law Review*. Vol. 74, pp. 399–49.

Hoff, David. 2008. Teacher-pay issue is hot in DNC discussions. *Education Week*. August 25.

Holmstrom, Bengt. 1982. Moral hazard in teams. *Bell Journal of Economics*. Vol. 13, pp. 324-40.

Jirjahn, Uwe. 2006. A note on efficiency wage theory and principal-agent theory. *Bulletin of Economic Research*. Forthcoming.

Jirjahn, Uwe. 2002. "The German Experience with Performance Pay." In Michelle Brown and John S. Heywood, eds., *Paying for Performance: An International Comparison*. Armonk N.Y.: M.E. Sharpe Publishers. pp.148–78.

Kandel, Eugene, and Edward P. Lazear. 1992. Peer pressure and partnerships. *Journal of Political Economy*. Vol. 100, pp. 801–17.

Kerr, Steven. 1975. On the folly of rewarding for A while hoping for B. *Academy of Management Journal.* Vol. 18. pp. 769–83.

Kessler, I. and J. Purcell. 1992. Performance related pay: Objectives and application. *Human Resource Management Journal.* Vol. 2, pp. 16–33.

Kim, Dong-One. 1999. Determinants of the survival of gainsharing programs. *Industrial and Labor Relations Review.* Vol. 51, pp. 21–42.

Khalil, Fahad, and Jacques Lawaree. 1995. Input versus output monitoring: Who is the residual claimant? *Journal of Economic Theory.* Vol. 66, pp. 139–57.

Laffont, Jean Jacques. 1990. Analysis of hidden gaming in a three-level hierarchy. *Journal of Law, Economics, and Organization.* Vol. 6, pp. 301–24.

Lawler, Edward E. 2003. Pay practices in Fortune 100 corporations. *World at Work Journal.* Vol. 12, No. 4, pp. 45–54.

Lazear, Edward P. 2000. Performance pay and productivity. *American Economic Review.* Vol. 90, pp. 1346–61.

Lazear, Edward P. 1986. Salaries and piece rates. *Journal of Business.* Vol. 59, pp. 405–31.

Lee, Christopher. 2005. Bush aims to expand system of merit pay. *Washington Post*, July 19, 2005, pp. A02.

Lemieux, Thomas, W. Bentley Macleod, and Daniel Parent. 2007. "Performance pay and wage inequality." NBER Working Paper, No. 13128. Cambridge, Mass.: NBER.

Levine, David I. 1992. Piece rates, output restriction, and conformism. *Journal of Economic Psychology.* Vol. 13, pp. 473-89.

Lewin, David., and Mitchell, Daniel J.B. 1995. *Human Resource Management: An Economic Approach* (2nd ed.). Cincinnati, Ohio: South-Western.

MacDonald, Glenn and Leslie M. Marx. 2001. Adverse specialization. *Journal of Political Economy.* Vol. 109, pp. 864–99.

Milgrom, Paul, and John Roberts. 1990. The economics of modern manufacturing: technology, strategy, and organization. *American Economic Review.* Vol. 80, pp. 511–28.

Milkovich, G.T., and J.M. Newman. 2002. *Compensation* (7th ed). Boston: McGraw-Hill Irwin.

Milkovich , G.T., and A.K. Widgor. 1991. *Pay for Performance: Evaluating Performance Appraisal and Merit Pay.* Washington D.C.: National Academy Press.

Parent, D. 2004. Incentives? The effect of profit sharing plans offered by previous employers on current wages. *Economics Letters.* Vol. 83, pp. 37–42.

Pfeffer, Jeffrey. 1998. Six dangerous myths about pay. *Harvard Business Review*. Vol. 76, No. 3, 108–119.

Pfuntner, Jordan. 2004. New benefits data. *Monthly Labor Review*. Vol. 127, pp. 6–21.

Prendergast, Canice. 2002. The tenuous trade-off between risk and incentives. *Journal of Political Economy*. Vol. 110, pp. 1071-102.

Prendergast, Canice. 1999. The provision of incentives in firms. *Journal of Economic Literature*. Vol. 37, pp. 7-63.

Prendergast, Canice. 1993. A theory of yes men. *American Economic Review*. Vol. 83, pp. 757-770.

Prendergast, Canice, and Robert H. Topel. 1996. Favoritism in organizations. J*ournal of Political Economy*. Vol. 100, pp. 958–78.

Ruser, John W. 2001. The employment cost index: What is it? *Monthly Labor Review*. September 3.

Smith, Sharon. 1987. "Wages in the Public and Private Sector: Comment." In D. Wise, ed., *Public Sector Payrolls*. Chicago: University of Chicago Press.

Staiger, Douglas O., Robert Gordon, Thomas J. Kane. 2006. "Identifying effective teachers using performance on the job." The Hamilton Project, Working Paper 2006-01, Washington, D.C.: Brookings Institution.

Tatsumichi, Shingo, and Motohito Morishima. 2007. *Seikashugi* from an employee perspective. *Japan Labor Review*. Vol. 4, No. 2, pp. 79–104.

Van het Karr, Robert, and Marianne Gruenell. 2001. "Variable pay in Europe." European Industrial Relations Observatory, European Foundation for the Improvement of Living and Working Conditions, viewed online, March 22, 2005:   www.eiro.eurofound.eu.int/about/2001/04/study/tn0104201s.html

Weitzman, M. 1984. *The Share Economy*. Cambridge Mass.: Harvard University Press.

PART II ———————————————————

The Perils of Quantitative Performance Accountability

by Richard Rothstein

Introduction

Teachers are an important resource schools contribute to their students' educational outcomes, and state and federal policy makers are attempting to find new ways to attract and retain talent in the classroom. A now-popular proposal is the use of performance-based, or "merit" pay for teachers—the tying of an individual teacher's salary to changes in her students' standardized test performance. Many commentators argue that such a link will not only incentivize teachers to focus on student outcomes, but will also radically transform the teacher labor market by drawing more talent into teaching.

Paying teachers, or for that matter any employee, for outcomes we value has considerable intuitive appeal. However, a closer look reveals that in many sectors of the economy, including education, a naïve application of accountability mechanisms, incentives, and pay-for-performance is fraught with danger. As Herbert A. Simon, winner of the Nobel Prize in economics, argued: weighing measurable costs and benefits does "not even remotely describe the processes that human beings use for making decisions in complex situations" (Simon 1978, 366).

Undaunted by such caution, policy makers have recently devised quantitative incentive systems to maximize public service efficiency. In Great Britain, Margaret Thatcher attempted to rationalize public enterprises: where they could not be privatized, her government hoped to regulate them using rewards and sanctions for quantifiable outcomes. Tony Blair accelerated these efforts, while in the United States, the Clinton administration proposed to similarly "reinvent government." The Government Performance Results Act of 1993 (GPRA) demanded a shift in attention from processes toward measurable outcomes.

These efforts took little account of Herbert Simon's insights and ignored warnings of the great methodologist, Donald T. Campbell, who concluded that attempts to reward institutional behavior should account for actors who behaved differently when they were being measured.

Social scientists have long been aware of possible Hawthorne effects, so named because factory workers apparently behaved differently when being studied. Almost a Heisenberg uncertainty principle for human behavior, the Hawthorne effect suggests it is difficult to get human beings to "stand still" long enough for their activity to be measured. At the Hawthorne Electric factory in the 1920s, workers simply stepped up efforts when they were studied (both when their work areas were made brighter and dimmer), perhaps to make themselves look better to social scientists.

But Hawthorne workers had no personal stake in the research findings, no financial or security incentives to trick observers into believing performance was better than, in fact, it typically was. Donald Campbell, however, was concerned not with social science research generally but with accountability and control systems specifically. In these, possibilities of rewards or punishments create incentives for agents to appear more competent, even employing deception and fraud to improve the impression. In 1979, Campbell framed what he called a "law" of performance measurement:

> The more any quantitative social indicator is used for social decision-making, the more subject it will be to corruption pressures and the more apt it will be to distort and corrupt the social processes it is intended to monitor. (Campbell 1979, 85)[1]

The law summarized efforts to use quantitative output indicators not only in education, but also in business, health care, welfare policy, human capital development, criminal justice, and public administration.

Simon and Campbell defined two shoals on which public accountability policy has foundered: that public goals are too complex to reduce to simple quantifiable measures; and attempts to do so corrupt public service.

As policy makers in education now grapple with consequences of No Child Left Behind (NCLB), they should keep in mind the three obstacles they face while implementing incentive mechanisms such as merit pay for teachers:

1. Conventional definitions and measurements of educational *outputs* are so over-simplified that they cannot support valid accountability or performance incentive systems. Goal *distortion* results, including re-allocation of resources to tested curricular areas from non-tested areas (like art, music, science, social studies, or physical education); and increased focus of math and reading instruction on more easily tested "basic" skills, with decreased focus on less-easily tested "higher order" skills.

2. Adjusting expectations of performance for the characteristics of *inputs* has proven more difficult than anticipated. With students at different risks of failure because of their varied background characteristics, accountability and incentive systems can be credible only if sanctions and rewards can be adjusted for these variations. *Defining subgroups* and measuring their performances separately is one way, but educators have neither determined how to tailor expectations by subgroup nor determined how to prevent cream-skimming. With school choice expanding, and subgroup definitions broad, do some schools and teachers meet public expectations by the subtle selection from at-risk subgroups of those students who are least at risk?

3. *Untrustworthy statistics* undermine the credibility of accountability and incentive systems. They would do so even if measurement of outputs and inputs could be

defined more precisely. Inadequate *data reliability* is one impediment: relying on a single annual test of relatively small student cohorts in schools, NCLB tolerates large confidence intervals in score reporting—this problem will be exacerbated in a merit pay system for individual teachers. To avoid misidentifying some low performers, others may be overlooked.[2] Because standardized test items are too few to fully represent the curriculum, *sampling corruption* results. Teachers and schools can game accountability by over-emphasizing skills needed to answer unrepresentative test questions.

These challenges—in defining outputs and inputs and in the accuracy of data themselves—surprise many education policy makers who often blame it on the inadequacy of public educators. In fact, however, the corruption of performance incentive systems stimulated by a too-heavy reliance on quantitative measurement is not peculiar to public education. It has been extensively documented in other fields by economists, business management theorists, sociologists, and historians. This portion of this volume hopes to familiarize students of performance incentives in education with this voluminous literature from other fields. It reviews evidence from medical care, job training, crime control, and other human services regarding corruption similar to what is now being encountered in public education: mismeasurement of outputs (goal distortion, and threshold standards that harmfully redirect effort); mismeasurement of inputs (imprecise subgroup definitions and cream-skimming); and untrustworthy statistics (data unreliability, sampling corruption, and other forms of gaming).[3]

This second part of the book also discusses how these problems limit the use of performance incentives in the private sector, and concludes by showing that performance incentives run the risk of subverting the intrinsic motivation of agents in service professions like teaching.

Accountability by the Numbers

In 1935, a 19-year-old political science major at the University of Chicago interviewed Milwaukee city administrators for a term paper. He was puzzled that when money became available to invest in parks, school board and public works officials could not agree on whether to hire more playground supervisors or improve physical maintenance of the parks themselves. He concluded that rational decision making was impossible because "improving parks" included multiple goals: school board members thought mostly of recreational opportunities for children, while public works administrators thought mostly of green space to reduce urban density.

The next year, the director of the International City Managers' Association hired the young graduate as a research assistant. Together they reviewed techniques for evaluating municipal services, including police, fire, public health, education, libraries, parks, and public works. Their 1938 book, *Measuring Municipal Activities*, concluded that quantitative measures of performance were mostly inappropriate because public services have goals that cannot easily be defined in simple numerical terms.

The senior author, Clarence E. Ridley, directed the city managers' association until retiring in 1956. His assistant, Herbert A. Simon, went on to win the Nobel Prize in economics for a lifetime of work demonstrating that organizational behavior is characterized by "bounded rationality." In *Measuring Municipal Activities*, Ridley and Simon observed that public services have multiple purposes and, even if precise definitions for some purposes were possible, evaluating the services overall would require difficult judgments about which purposes were relatively more important. Also, it was never possible to quantify whether outcome differences between cities were attributable to differences in effort and competence of public employees, or to differences in the conditions—difficult to measure in any event —under which agencies worked. The authors concluded that "[t]he most serious single problem which still stands in the way of the development of satisfactory measurement techniques is the difficulty of defining the objectives of municipal services in measurable terms" (Ridley and Simon 1938 and 1943, vii). Objectives, for example, like "improve health...or develop good citizens must be stated in much more tangible and objective terms before they adapt themselves to measurement" (Ridley and Simon 1938 and 1943, 2).

Ridley and Simon noted that, before attempting quantitative measurement, questions should be addressed such as: For evaluating library services, should judgments be made about the quality of books being circulated? (Ridley and Simon 1938 and 1943, 47-8). For a mortality index for public health, should all lives be considered equally valuable—those of the elderly, of very young children, and of productive workers? (Ridley and Simon 1938 and 1943, 26).

Ridley and Simon had something to say about measuring school effectiveness as well:

> The chief fault of the testing movement has consisted in its emphasis upon content in highly academic material....The fact that a particular pupil shows a marked improvement in reading or spelling may give some indication that a teacher is improving her performance...but the use to which the pupil puts that knowledge is the only significant point in determining the significance of subject tests in measuring the educational system. (Ridley and Simon 1938 and 1943, 43)

And:

> The final appraisal of the school system must be in terms of its impact upon the community through the individuals that it trains. How effective is the school system in raising the cultural level of the community?...What is the delinquency rate in the community?...Is the economic situation improving as a result of intelligent effort on the part of the people?...What is the proportion of registered voters to the eligible voting population?...
>
> From a practical standpoint, no one is so optimistic as to believe that all these results can be directly measured, but...serious attempts will be made in the future to devise measures which will approximate these end-products as closely as possible. (Ridley and Simon 1938 and 1943, 45)

There is today growing enthusiasm by politicians and policy makers for quantitative accountability systems that might maximize public service efficiency. But they have rushed to develop measurement systems without giving thought to whether these systems were truly measuring ultimate outcomes of the kind that Ridley and Simon described 70 years ago.

Enthusiasm for holding schools and teachers accountable for student test scores is but part of this broader trend that has proceeded oblivious to the warnings of Herbert Simon and other notable social scientists. Scholars have often concluded that, when agents in other sectors are held accountable for improving production of a simple numerical output, performance on that easily measured output does improve. But overall performance may deteriorate. So economists, sociologists, and management theorists generally caution against accountability systems that rely exclusively, or even primarily, on numerical outcome measures. Such corruption occurs primarily because of the problem Herbert Simon identified—an indicator that can be quantified often reflects only an aspect of the outcome of interest, so undue attention to this aspect will distort the balance of services being provided.

In his 1989 study, *Bureaucracy*, James Q. Wilson wondered why public agencies did not employ "carefully designed compensation plans" that would permit public employees to benefit, financially, from good performance. "Part of the answer," he said, "is obvious. Often we do not know whether a manager or an agency has achieved the goals we want because either the goals are vague or inconsistent, or their attainment cannot be observed, or both. Bureau chiefs in the Department of State would have to go on welfare if their pay depended on their ability to demonstrate convincingly that they had attained their bureaus' objectives" (Wilson 1989, 117). We could, of course, pay diplomats based on the number of dinners they attended because informal contacts with representatives of other nations should have a positive relationship to the goal of advancing the national interest. But if we did implement such a performance-based pay system, we might find that diplomats got fatter while the national interest was ignored.

Soviet Central Planning

Before the Soviet Union collapsed, Western scholarly and popular publications often reported about the goal distortion and corruption resulting from Soviet attempts to manage an economy by mandating the achievement of numerical output goals. State industrial planners established targets for enterprise production and punished managers who failed to meet them. For example, there were targets for the number of shoes to be produced. Certainly, increasing output was an important goal of the Soviet shoe industry, but it was not the only goal. Factories responded to the accountability requirements by using a limited leather supply to produce a glut of small sizes that consumers could not use. Planners specified the number of kilometers that freight transport enterprises should cover each month. Certainly, transporters who cover more distance can deliver more goods. But when distance itself was incentivized, haulers fulfilled quotas by driving circuitous routes (Nove 1964, 294). Planners specified the number of meters to be drilled each quarter by geological prospectors. Certainly, geologists who drill more holes should discover more oil. But when drilling became an end in itself, geologists fulfilled quotas by digging rather than by finding oil (Nove 1964, 289). (Geologists could not be held accountable for finding oil, because digging is completely within their control, success somewhat less so.) A cartoon in a Soviet satirical magazine showed managers of a nail factory admiring their goal fulfillment: suspended from a crane was a gigantic nail that extended across the entire length of the factory; this was the most efficient way for the plant to fulfill its monthly quota, expressed in weight, for nails produced (Mullen 1985, 165).

Some Soviet incentives retarded technological progress. Electrifying the vast country was an important economic objective, but creating incentives to increase output gave electricity managers no reason to reduce inefficiency from the loss of current in transmission (Mullen 1985, 165). Quotas for other industries set in tons created incentives to avoid developing lighter materials (Mullen 1985, 165).

Education parallels

Soviet experience with simple quantitative accountability has been duplicated in modern times, in education, and in other sectors. In *Grading Education* (Rothstein et al. 2008), I show how attempts to hold schools accountable for math and reading test scores have corrupted education by reducing the attention paid to other important curricular goals; by creating incentives to ignore students who are either above or far below the passing point on tests; by misidentifying failing and successful schools because of test unreliability; by converting instruction into test preparation that has little lasting value; and by gaming, which borders (or may include) illegality.

Each of these corruptions has parallels in other fields, often studied and reported by social scientists and management theorists. But education policy makers have paid little attention to this expertise.[4] Instead, state and federal governments adopted test-based accountability as the tool for improving student achievement, duplicating the worst features of flawed accountability systems in other public and private services.

Some advocates of test-based accountability in education, confronted with evidence of goal distortion or excessive test preparation, have concluded that these problems stem only from the inadequacy of teachers. As one critic argues, good teachers "can and should" integrate subject matter so that raising math and reading scores need not result in diminished attention to other curricular areas (West 2007, 57). But this expectation denies the intent and power of incentives that, if successful, *should* redirect attention and resources to those outputs that are rewarded. The consistency with which professionals and their institutions respond in this fashion in all fields should persuade us that this is not a problem with the ethos of teachers, but an inevitable consequence of any narrowly quantitative incentive system.

Familiar examples

Body counts, ticket quotas, television sweeps, best-seller lists, college rankings, crime clearance rates, and Nixon's war on crime

Donald Campbell observed that a tragic example of goal distortion from quantifiable accountability stemmed from the work of a former Harvard Business School professor, financial analyst, and business-executive-turned-public-official. During the Vietnam War, Secretary of Defense Robert McNamara believed strongly in quantitative measures of success and demanded reports from his generals of American and North Vietnamese "body counts." It is true that just as high reading test scores are usually a reliable indicator of reading proficiency, relative casualties are usually a reliable indicator of the fortunes of a nation at war; a strong inverse correlation between a nation's casualties and its success in the broader political and economic objectives of warfare should normally be expected. But an army can be corrupted if imposing or avoiding casualties become ends in themselves, and if local commanders' performances are judged by this relatively easily measured indicator. Generals or civilian leaders may then lose sight of political and economic objectives. In the Vietnam War, American generals attempted to please their superiors by recording more enemy deaths than their own. As it was impossible to hide American deaths from political leaders, generals found ways to inflate the numbers of enemy deaths. In some cases, death became an end in itself, in other cases the categorization of deaths was corrupted (for example, by counting civilian as enemy deaths) or the numbers simply exaggerated. High enemy body count numbers led American leaders to believe the war was being won. These leaders confused superiority in body counts with achievement of political and economic objectives. The war was then lost (Campbell 1979, 86).

Other unfortunate consequences of quantitative accountability are familiar. Motorists stopped by police for trivial traffic violations may have experienced an accountability system in which police sergeants evaluate officers by whether they meet ticket quotas. Certainly, issuing citations for traffic violations is one measure of good policing, but when officers are disproportionately judged by this easily quantifiable outcome, they have incentives to focus on trivial offenses that meet a quota, rather than investigating more serious crimes where the payoff may be less certain. The numerical accountability system generates false arrests, and creates incentives for police officers to boost their measured productivity by disregarding suspects' rights. In New York City a few years ago, the use of quantifiable indicators to measure police productivity resulted in the publicized (and embarrassing, to the police) arrest of an 80-year-old man for feeding pigeons and of a pregnant woman for sitting down to rest on a subway stairway (Murray 2005).

Management theorists and criminologists have long decried the quota practice, but police departments continue to be seduced by an apparently easy way to ensure that officers do not waste excessive time on coffee breaks (Deming 1986, 104; Uhlig 1987; Jackman 2004; Moore 2007). In 1966, the criminologist Jerome Skolnick wrote, "The goals of police and the standards by which the policeman's work is to be evaluated are ambiguous....Even within the ranks of police specialists there is no clear understanding of goals," making judgment based on simple quantitative indicators bound to distort police priorities (Skolnick 1966, 164).

Television programming offers another example of Campbell's law. Stations sell advertising at rates throughout the year determined by viewership during three designated "sweeps" months, November, February, and May. A survey company (Nielsen) sends surveys to a sample of viewers during these months to determine what programs typical viewers watch. The system assumes that sweeps-month programming is representative of programming throughout the year for which advertising is sold. Yet the stations respond to these high-stakes surveys by scheduling programs during sweeps months that are more popular, or attention-grabbing, than those of a typical month. Some stations even award cash prizes to viewers who watch programs at times the survey is being conducted (Farhi 1996). Certainly, viewership numbers at sampled times should reflect whether station programming is likely to draw viewers. But when viewership numbers become ends in themselves, they distort and corrupt the processes they are intended to monitor.

Several newspapers, most notably the *New York Times*, publish weekly best-seller lists. Books on the list get special displays and promotions in book stores, resulting in substantial increases in sales (and authors' royalties). The best-seller list is compiled from computerized reports sent to the *Times* from a national sample of bookstores. But publishers attempt to "teach to the test," identifying which book stores are going to be sampled and organizing bulk purchases, thereby bumping the book up to the best-seller list. The *Times*, not always successfully, monitors book store sales to identify such artificial purchases that corrupt the representativeness of the index. "People do try to game the list," the editor in charge has acknowledged (Hoyt 2007).

U.S. News and World Report publishes an annual ranking of colleges. The rankings are truly an accountability system; many college boards of trustees consider the rankings when determining presidential compensation. In at least one case, a university president (at Arizona State) was offered a large bonus if the university's ranking moved up on his watch (Jaschik 2007).

U.S. News rankings are based on several factors, including the judgments of college presidents and other administrators about the quality of their peer institutions, and the selectiveness of a college, determined partly by the percentage of applicants who are admitted (a more selective college admits a smaller percentage of applicants). Thus, the rankings are a candidate for illustration of Campbell's law, because these factors would be quite reasonable if there were no stakes attached to measuring them. College presidents and other administrators are in the best position to know the strengths and weaknesses of institutions similar to their own, and asking them for their opinions about this should be a good way to find out about college quality. But once an accountability rating is based on these answers, presidents have incentives to dissemble by giving competing institutions poorer ratings and making their own institutions appear relatively superior.

Likewise, higher-quality colleges are likely to accept relatively fewer applicants because demand for admission is strong. But once this indicator became an accountability measure, colleges had incentives to recruit applicants who were bound ultimately to be rejected. Colleges, for example, have sent promotional mailings to unqualified applicants and waived application fees in order to attract unsuccessful (and unsuspecting) applicants. The indicator nonetheless persists in *U.S. News* ratings, although it now has questionable value (Finder 2007).

The Federal Bureau of Investigation (FBI) tracks crime clearance rates to evaluate police departments' effectiveness. The clearance rate is the percentage of reported crimes that result in perpetrators' convictions. Just as high math scores characterize effective schools, high clearance rates characterize effective police departments. But as with math scores, once clearance rates become ends in themselves, Campbell's law sets in, and the indicator distorts and corrupts the social processes it is intended to monitor. Police can increase the clearance rate by offering reduced charges to suspects who confess to other crimes, even those they may not actually have committed. Such plea bargains give detectives big boosts in their clearance rates. Meanwhile, those who plead guilty only to the crime for which they were arrested typically get harsher penalties than those who make false confessions to multiple crimes.

Incentives to raise clearance rates are commonplace, although this use of a numerical measure undermines justice—the true, and difficult to quantify, objective of law enforcement (Skolnick 1966, 176 and 181).

As a 1968 presidential candidate, Richard M. Nixon promised a "war" on crime. After his election, the FBI publicly reported crime statistics by city. It judged whether police departments were effective by the sum of crimes in seven categories: murder, forcible rape, robbery, aggravated assault, burglary, auto theft, and serious larceny (defined as theft resulting in a loss of at least $50). Many cities subsequently posted significant reductions in crime (Seidman and Couzens 1974). But the crime reductions were apparently realized by playing with crime classifications. The biggest reductions were in larcenies of $50 and over in value. Valuing larceny is a matter of judgment, so police departments placed lower values on reported losses after the implementation of the accountability system than before (Seidman and Couzens 1974, 462). Although the number of alleged $50 larcenies (which counted for accountability purposes) declined, the number of alleged $49 larcenies (which did not count) increased.

Policemen nationwide were under orders to downgrade the classification of crimes to show progress in their cities' crime index numbers (Morrissey 1972; Twigg 1972). Donald Campbell concluded: "It seems to be well-documented that a well-publicized, deliberate effort at social change—Nixon's crackdown on crime—had as its main effect the corruption of crime-rate indicators, achieved through under-recording and by downgrading the crimes to less serious classifications" (Campbell 1979, 85).[5]

A not-so-familiar example

Santiago bus drivers

A curious example of goal distortion that arises from setting a purely quantitative standard for public services comes from the bus system of Santiago, Chile. Most bus drivers worldwide are paid a flat wage. And almost everywhere, passengers complain of waiting too long for a bus to come, only to have several arrive together. To prevent this, Santiago pays most (but not all) bus drivers per passenger carried. In establishing this system, the authorities reasoned that if bus drivers were accountable for the number of passengers carried, and drivers found themselves too close to the previous bus, they would slow down to give additional passengers time to congregate at bus stops. The result would be better service from more evenly spaced buses.

The system works: typical Santiago passengers wait 13% longer for buses whose drivers are paid a flat rate than for those whose drivers are paid per passenger. But instead of slowing down to allow passengers to congregate at stops, incentive-drivers speed up, to pass buses in front and thus collect passengers before other drivers do so. Drivers accountable for the number of passengers have 67% more accidents per mile than fixed-wage drivers. Passengers complain that buses on incentive contracts lurch forward as soon as passengers board, without their having a chance to sit (Johnson, Reiley, and Munoz 2006).

Bus drivers have to balance several goals—delivering passengers rapidly to their destinations, safety, and comfort. By creating an accountability and compensation system based only on a more easily measured output, Santiago bus companies undermined other goals.

Goal distortion in health care report cards

Quantitative accountability has corrupted aspects of health care, both in Great Britain and the United States. Heart surgery is an example in both countries. Beginning in the late 1980s, both national governments (and several American states) hoped to persuade patients to choose more effective care, especially because public funds (Medicare and Medicaid in the United States) might otherwise be wasted. So the governments created "report cards" to compare the extent to which patients of different doctors and hospitals survived open-heart surgery. Goal distortion resulted.

Health care, like education, has multiple goals that providers must balance. For heart patients, one goal is certainly to prolong life. But a second is to respect wishes of terminally ill patients who choose to avoid artificial life-prolonging technology and hope for a more dignified experience when death is inevitable. To this end, federal legislation requires hospitals to provide patients with information about living wills. The two goals are difficult to balance and can be reconciled only by the judgments in specific cases of the physicians and families involved. Heart surgery report cards undermined this balancing process. By rewarding hospitals only for reducing easily measured mortality rates, accountability systems created incentives to ignore the other goal of encouraging appropriate use of living wills (Green, Passman, and Wintfield 1991, 853).

Britain's National Health Service (NHS) also ran up against Campbell's law when it attempted to compare the performance of maternity services so that it could encourage mothers to use those of higher quality. To this end, NHS published comparative data on providers' perinatal mortality rates—the rate of infant deaths immediately before and after birth. This is certainly the most easily quantifiable outcome of obstetrics. But there are other objectives as well, including reducing the severity of handicaps with which high-risk infants survive, and providing a more comfortable and competent experience for pregnant mothers.

These more difficult-to-quantify objectives require maternity services to devote more resources to prenatal care. The incentive system, publishing only the quantifiable perinatal mortality rate, led maternity services to re-balance their efforts between community-based prenatal care and hospital deliveries. With limited resources, maternity services invested less in prenatal care so they could invest more in hospital services. The perinatal mortality rate declined, just as the incentive system intended. But there were worse developmental outcomes for live births—more low birthweight babies and more children born who later had learning difficulties and behavioral problems—because less attention had been paid to prenatal care (Smith 1993, 141-42).

NHS also established a standard that no patient should wait more than two years for elective surgery. This created incentives for surgeons to perform more operations and spend less time on post-operative care, which was unmeasured in the accountability system (Smith 1993, 146-47). Such a shift may have reduced overall patient welfare. Because surgical urgency is on a continuum, not neatly divided between elective and urgent procedures, the target for elective surgery caused practitioners to make relatively minor procedures (some cataract surgeries, for example) a greater priority and more serious but not quite urgent procedures a lesser priority; in that way all surgeries could be performed within the target time frame (Goddard, Mannion, and Smith 2000, 141-42, 149). A consequence was that *average* waiting times for surgery increased, even though more surgeries were performed within two years (Smith 1995, 291).

In 2002, following highly publicized cases of mistreatment of the elderly in nursing homes, the Health Care Financing Administration (HCFA, now renamed the Centers for Medicaid and Medicare Services, or CMS) established a report card, the Nursing Home Quality Initiative (NHQI), which required nursing homes to report publicly whether they adhered to 15 recognized quality standards—for example, the percent of residents who have pressure sores (from being turned in bed too infrequently). These public reports were intended to provide information about relative quality to consumers who were selecting nursing homes for themselves or elderly relatives. However, administrators of nursing homes, and nurses caring for the elderly, must balance many more than these 15 aspects of quality. For example, because nurses' time is limited, if they spend more time turning patients in bed (an NHQI standard), they may have less time to maintain hygienic standards by washing their hands regularly (not an NHQI standard). Although the NHQI was intended to be easily understood by consumers and is limited to 15 standards, CMS monitors some 190 measures (such as hand washing) on a checklist when it inspects nursing homes for purposes of certifying eligibility for Medicaid or Medicare reimbursement. Following the introduction of NHQI, performance on the 15 selected indicators improved, but adherence to the 190 standards overall declined, resulting in more citations for violations issued by CMS (Lu 2007). Infections from less hand washing by nurses increased.

In 1994, the U.S. General Accounting Office (GAO) published an analysis of health care report cards. It concluded: "[A]dministrators will place all their organizations' resources in areas that are being measured. Areas that are not highlighted in report cards will be ignored" (GAO 1994, 55).

Risk adjustment

Test-based accountability systems in education should (though often do not) adjust results for differences in student characteristics. A school with large numbers of low-income children, high residential mobility, great family stress, little literacy support at home, and serious health problems may be a better school even if its test scores are lower than another whose pupils do not have such challenges; similarly for teachers.

Education policy makers sometimes try to adjust for these differences by comparing only "similar" schools and teachers—those, for example, with similar proportions of minority students, or similar proportions of students who are low income (eligible for the federal free and reduced-price lunch program).

But this solution does not really solve the problem. Stable working class families, with incomes nearly double the poverty line, are eligible for the federal lunch program; schools with such students can easily get higher scores than schools with very poor students, yet the latter schools may be more effective. Charter schools can enroll minority students whose parents are more highly motivated than those in neighborhood schools, tempting charter school promoters to make false claims of superiority when their test scores are higher (Carnoy et al. 2005).

The difficulty of adjusting for differences in unmeasured background characteristics was identified by Clarence Ridley and Herbert Simon in their 1938 study of municipal functions. To compare the effectiveness of fire departments in different cities or years, they found it impossible to use simple quantitative measures, such as the annual value of fire losses or the number of fires per capita. From one year or place to another, there might be a change in the amount of burnable property or in the proportion of industrial property, a more severe winter that might lead to greater use of flammable materials within buildings, or "a multitude of other factors beyond the control of the administrator [that] would have an important effect upon the loss rate" (Ridley and Simon 1938 and 1943, 3).

And Ridley and Simon considered fire the easiest of municipal activities to measure (Ridley and Simon 1938 and 1943, 10). Comparisons of police effectiveness, they argued, had to account not only for racial and ethnic differences in populations but also the quality of housing, economic conditions, the availability of "wholesome recreational facilities," the administration of the courts, and "other intangible factors of civic morale" (Ridley and Simon 1938 and 1943). Evaluation of public health workers' performance had to adjust for similar factors, as well as for climate, epidemics, and other chance fluctuations in population health. Construction of a mortality index for measuring the adequacy of public health departments must distinguish "only those diseases which are partly or wholly preventable through public health measures" (Ridley and Simon 1938 and 1943, 28).

Medicine faces similar problems; some patients are much sicker, and thus harder to cure, than others with the same disease. Patients' ages, other diseases, history of prior treatment, health habits (smoking, for example), diet, and home environment must all be taken into account. So before comparing outcome data, health care report cards must be "risk-adjusted" for the initial conditions of patients. Although risk adjustment in medicine is far more sophisticated than controls for minority status or lunch eligibility in education, health policy experts still consider that the greatest flaw in medical accountability systems is their inability to adjust performance comparisons adequately for patient characteristics.

The Health Care Financing Administration (HCFA) initiated its accountability system for cardiac surgery in 1986 with its reports on death rates of Medicare patients in 5,500 U.S. hospitals. HCFA used a complex statistical model to identify hospitals whose death rates after surgery were greater than expected, after accounting for patient characteristics. Yet the institution labeled as having the worst death rate, even after sophisticated risk-adjustment, turned out to be a hospice caring for terminally ill patients (Iezzoni 1994, 40).

The following year, HCFA added even more patient characteristics to its statistical model. Although the agency now insisted that its model adequately adjusted for all critical variables, the ratings invariably resulted in higher adjusted mortality rates for low-income patients in urban hospitals than for affluent patients in suburban hospitals (Schick 2001, 41). Campbell's law swung into action—when surveyed, physicians and hospitals began to admit that they were refusing to treat sicker patients (Casalino et al. 2007, 495). Surgeons' ratings were not adversely affected by deaths of patients who had been denied surgery. Surveys of cardiologists found that most were declining to operate on patients who might benefit from surgery but were of greater risk (Santora 2005; Casalino et al. 2007, 496). Some hospitals, more skilled at selection, got higher ratings, while others did worse because they received a larger share of patients with more severe disease. In 1989, St. Vincent's Hospital in New York City was put on probation by the state after it placed low in the ranking of state hospitals for cardiac surgery. The following year, it ranked first in the state. St. Vincent's accomplished this feat by refusing to operate on tougher cases (Altman 1990).

Just as some schools that are failing in comparison to all schools may be judged satisfactory when compared only to similar schools, whether hospitals have unsatisfactory mortality rates depends on the particular risk-adjustment formula employed in the ratings. An analysis of gastrointestinal hemorrhage cases in Great Britain found successive revisions of hospital rankings as additional adjustments for patient characteristics were applied (McKee 1996, 430). A study of stroke victims in the United States applied 11 alternative (and commonly used) systems for measuring severity of risk and found that hospitals deemed better-than-average according to some systems were deemed worse-than-average according to others (Iezzoni et al. 1995).

HCFA's Medicare performance indicator system was abandoned in 1993. Bruce Vladeck, the HCFA administrator at that time, conceded that the methodology was flawed. "I think it's overly simplistic," he told an interviewer. "[I]t doesn't adequately adjust for some of the problems faced by inner-city hospitals" (Associated Press 1993). Added Jerome Kassirer, then editor-in-chief of the *New England Journal of Medicine*, "The public has a right to know about the quality of its doctors, yet…it is irresponsible to release information that is of questionable validity, subject to alternative interpretations, or too technical for a layperson to understand…." He concluded that "no practice profile [i.e., physician report card] in use today is adequate to [the] task" (Kassirer 1994).

In 1994, when the GAO published its health care report card study, several state incentive systems were still in place, as were some that had been devised by private insurers. The GAO found that no public or private report card had been able to develop a method to adjust for patient characteristics that was "valid and reliable"

(GAO 1994, 5-6). Kaiser Permanente in Northern California, for example, published a report card that included over 100 measures of performance (GAO 1994, 26). Yet the GAO observed that "each performance indicator may need its own separate adjustment because patient characteristics have a unique effect on every condition and disease" (GAO 1994, 42).

Similar problems arise when we attempt to adjust for risk factors in education—for example, family characteristics apparently have a more powerful impact on reading scores than on math scores, the latter being more sensitive to school quality and the former to family intellectual environment.

Gaming health care accountability

Quantitative accountability in health care has also inspired gamesmanship by providers not so different from the games educators have learned to play under test-based accountability plans. Obstetricians, for example, can never precisely define the date of conception, so in Britain, when they were held accountable for reducing mortality after a gestation cutoff of 28 weeks, obstetricians improved their performance indicators in borderline cases by reporting that mortality occurred before, not after, the 28-week cutoff (Smith 1993, 149).

Britain's NHS also established a target that no patient should sit in an emergency room for more than four hours before seeing a physician. Hospitals soon dramatically improved their consistency in meeting this threshold. But average waiting times sometimes also increased and health care deteriorated. Previously, the highly publicized cases that gave rise to the target were mostly patients with relatively minor injuries or illnesses who were forced to wait on the infrequent (but not unheard of) occasions when emergency rooms were overwhelmed by more serious cases. To meet the new accountability requirement, hospitals ensured that patients with less serious problems were seen before the four hours expired but, as a result, patients with more serious problems had to wait somewhat longer than they had previously. A review committee of the Royal Statistical Society concluded that the accountability target had undermined medical ethics that require treatment priority based on need (Bird et al. 2005, 20).

Moreover, because the four-hour waiting standard did not begin until patients actually arrived at an emergency room, some ambulances parked and did not discharge patients to the emergency room until advised that the hospital could now see a patient within four hours. This gaming had detrimental effects on the delivery of health care, as patients with relatively minor problems were not treated any sooner, but fewer ambulances were available for dispatch to pick up seriously ill patients (Bevan and Hood 2006, 531).

Another NHS standard was that patients should be able to see their primary care physicians within 48 hours of making appointments. Some physicians met this accountability threshold simply by refusing to schedule appointments more than 48 hours in advance (Bevan and Hood 2006, 523). When asked about this at a press conference,

Prime Minister Tony Blair said it was "absurd" to think that doctors would do such a thing, but his health secretary later confirmed that this was, indeed, a perverse consequence of the accountability target (Timmins 2005).

Medical data corruption is another kind of gaming that results from quantitative accountability systems. Many background characteristics used for risk adjustment must be coded by and collected from the physicians themselves who are being held accountable for risk-adjusted outcomes. Physicians have always used great discretion in coding. As the General Accounting Office (GAO) noted in its evaluation of health care report cards, many Americans have had the experience of friendly physicians who creatively code a routine office visit to qualify for insurance reimbursement. Physicians sometimes alter coding to protect patient privacy, masking diagnoses of alcoholism, HIV, or mental illness, for example (GAO 1994, 38). Thus it is no surprise that after incentive systems were put in place, physicians used their discretion to classify symptoms that patients initially present as more severe than the same symptoms would have been classified prior to the incentive system (McKee and Hunter 1994, 112; Smith 1993, 148). For example, after New York State began to report death rates from cardiac surgery, the share of cardiac patients reported by physicians to have serious risk factors prior to surgery rose dramatically. Patients reported also to suffer from chronic obstructive pulmonary disease more than doubled, and those reported to be suffering from renal failure jumped seven-fold (Green and Wintfeld 1995, Table 1). Since the definitions of many co-morbid conditions are not precise, it is unclear to what extent physicians consciously manipulated the data. Nonetheless, 41% of the reduction in New York's risk-adjusted mortality for cardiac bypass patients was attributable to the apparently artificial increase ("upcoding") in reported severity of patients' conditions (Green and Wintfeld 1995, Epstein 1995).

In 2003, a team of American health care economists published an analysis of health care report cards. Their academic paper concluded that report cards on health care providers "may give doctors and hospitals incentives to decline to treat more difficult, severely ill patients." The accountability system has "led to higher levels of resource use [because delaying surgery for sicker patients necessitated more expensive treatment later] and to worse outcomes, particularly for sicker patients....[A]t least in the short-run, these report cards decreased patient and social welfare" (Dranove et al. 2003, 555-56, 557).

One of the paper's co-authors was Mark McClellan, who had been a member of President George W. Bush's Council of Economic Advisers while *No Child Left Behind* was designed and implemented. The paper concluded that, although report cards advertised that some hospitals got dramatically better outcomes, "On net, these changes were particularly harmful....Report cards on the performance of schools raise the same issues and therefore also need empirical evaluation" (Dronove et al. 2003, 583-85).

Dr. McClellan subsequently served as administrator of the Centers for Medicare and Medicaid Services from 2004 to 2006. Apparently ignoring his earlier conclusions, the federal government reinstituted Medicare accountability report cards in 2007, publishing the names of 41 hospitals with higher-than-expected death rates for heart attack patients.

The government planned next to add a report card for pneumonia. The Bush administration's Secretary of Health and Human Services, Michael Leavitt, acknowledged that the list of failing hospitals still imperfectly adjusted for patient characteristics, but promised that "[i]t will get nothing but better as time goes on" (Harris 2007).

Ignoring McClellan's conclusions, six states continue to publish report cards on cardiac surgery mortality rates in their hospitals, and three publish performance reports for individual surgeons (Steinbrook 2006).

Accountability in job training and welfare

In 1955, the organizational sociologist Peter M. Blau studied a state employment agency's tasks of registering jobless workers for benefits and providing assistance in finding new jobs. Initially, Blau found that the state attempted to hold case workers accountable by rating them according to the number of interviews they conducted. But this resulted in goal distortion; case workers had incentives to sacrifice quality for speed. So the state added seven new quantitative indicators, including the number of job referrals and actual placements, and the ratio of placements to interviews. Even these quantitative indicators were still deemed insufficient to balance all aspects of effective performance, so the agency prohibited supervisors from basing more than 40% of an employee's evaluation on quantitative indicators (Blau 1955, 38-42; 45-46).

The government has frequently attempted to impose accountability systems on job training and welfare agencies that use federal funds. As in health care, Campbell's law usually wins out: the reliance on quantitative indicators distorts and corrupts the agency functions that these indicators hope to monitor.

Under the Job Training Partnership Act (JTPA) of 1982, the government offered financial rewards to agencies that had better records of placing workers in jobs. The Department of Labor defined successful placements as those that lasted at least 90 days. This created incentives for agencies to place workers in low-skilled and short-term jobs that might last not much longer than 90 days (Courty, Heinrich, and Marschke 2005, 338).Training for long-term stable employment required more resources, and success rates in that area were somewhat lower, although placement in long-term stable employment was an important though unmeasured JTPA goal. The federal program could have reduced goal distortion by extending the monitoring program beyond 90 days, but the Department of Labor could not afford the additional expense (Stecher and Kirby 2004, 54, citing Courty and Marschke 1997, 384).

When JTPA rewarded agencies for the share of clients who were placed in jobs, it provided perverse incentives to recruit and train only those unemployed workers who were most easy to place, that is, workers who had been unemployed for only a short period, had the best skills or educational credentials, or favored race or ethnic backgrounds (Barnow and Smith 2004, 258-59). In these ways, the law's purpose to provide training to workers who "are most in need of training opportunities" was subverted (Barnow and Smith 2004, 249). James Heckman, a Nobel laureate in economics, concluded that JTPA "performance standards based on short-term outcome levels likely

do little to encourage the provision of services to those who benefit most from them…"
(Heckman, Heinrich, and Smith 2002, 808; Blalock and Barnow 2001, 505).

Gaming job training and welfare accountability

Accountability under the job training program created many opportunities for gaming.
Placements (or lack of them) were counted only for job seekers formally enrolled in
training programs. This counting method gave agencies incentives to train clients
informally, then formally enroll them only after it was determined that the job seekers
were certain to find employment. In other cases, because employment was verified 90
days after the end of formal training, agencies failed to graduate and continued
"formally training" some clients who had little hope of finding employment, long after
any hope for success had evaporated. Such gaming behavior continued under the Workforce Investment Act (WIA) of 1998, the JTPA successor program (Barnow and Smith
2004, 269-70). As the General Accounting Office observed, "[t]he lack of a uniform
understanding of when registration occurs and thus who should be counted toward the
measures raises questions about both the accuracy and comparability of states' performance data" (Barnow and Smith 2004, 269-70; GAO 2002, 17).

In some cases, agencies provided special services to support employment, such as
child care, transportation, or clothing allowances. Such services were often terminated
after the 90th day of employment. Similarly, case managers followed up with employers
and urged them to keep recent trainees on the payroll. Follow-up often ended on the
90th day. Such gaming did not take place prior to JTPA's establishment of a 90-day
standard for measuring performance (Barnow and Smith 2004, 271-72, citing Courty
and Marschke 1997).

The accountability plans of both JTPA and WIA required local agencies to demonstrate continuous performance improvement each year. As with education's NCLB, the
law recognized that conditions differed from state to state, so states were permitted to
establish their own target levels. As a result, many states established deliberately low
initial targets for their training agencies, to ensure more room for subsequent improvement (Courty, Heinrich, and Marschke 2005, 331, 341-42). This too anticipated states'
behavior in education, where many would attempt to meet NCLB proficiency standards
by defining proficiency at a level far below "challenging." Public administration theory
refers to this behavior as the "ratchet effect," a term taken from analyses of similar
behavior in the Soviet economy.

As in health care, the inability to adjust performance expectations adequately for
background characteristics has also frustrated accountability designs in job training and
welfare programs.

Following adoption of the 1996 welfare reform law, Temporary Assistance to
Needy Families (TANF), most states hired private contractors to administer at least
some aspects of the program. Wisconsin Works (W-2) was the state program most
frequently cited as a national model. The program rewarded private contractors on the
basis of participants' employment rate, average wage rate, job retention and quality

(whether employers provided health insurance), and educational activities (Heinrich and Choi 2007, 418 and Appendix). However, because Wisconsin's contracts did not employ risk-adjustments for economic conditions or recipients' relevant qualifications (for example, whether they had high school diplomas), contractors discouraged enroll-ment of the harder-to-serve cases, and contractors' profits were excessive. Every two years, Wisconsin redefined the incentive criteria to account for changes in economic conditions and in contractors' opportunistic selection of clients; otherwise, meeting the state's accountability requirements would have become even easier. After six years of this, Wisconsin gave up, eliminating performance standards and even rescinding bonus money that had been awarded (Heinrich and Marschke 2007, 21-23). And the federal government has discontinued using quantitative incentive systems to manage TANF programs in all states (Weisman 2007).[6]

Unlike TANF, the JTPA, and WIA job training programs employed statistical adjustments to account for some local agencies having an easier time placing the unemployed in jobs. If accurate adjustments were not made, agencies located in areas with booming economies, or where unemployed workers were more likely to have high school diplomas, could post better placement numbers than agencies in depressed areas with more high school dropouts. Nonetheless, despite the Department of Labor's relatively sophisticated attempts at risk-adjustment, the General Accounting Office found that subtle differences in local economic conditions—growth in new or existing businesses, for example—were not captured by the statistical models. Thus, the incen-tive system still encouraged agencies to select only those unemployed workers who were easiest to place (Courty, Heinrich, and Marschke 2005, 340, 342, and 336-37; Heinrich 2004; GAO 2002, 9 and 14). The GAO concluded: "Unless the performance levels can be adjusted to truly reflect differences in economic conditions and the population served, local areas will continue to have a disincentive to serve some job seekers that could be helped" (GAO 2002, 28).

Federal job training regulations also attempted to make accountability requirements sensitive to the population served by requiring the reporting of enrollment separately by subgroups, much as in education, where results are reported separately for minority and low-income students. Unlike education, however, where contemporary accountability programs require all students to achieve the same level of performance, each subgroup of job seekers had a unique target, considered appropriate for its unique challenges; the handicapped, racial minorities, and welfare recipients each had specific training targets. However, these categories were too broad to defeat the ability of counselors to distinguish potentially more successful trainees from within these targeted groups (e.g., blacks and welfare recipients who were relatively more able than others). Those with more education were disproportionately recruited for training (Courty, Heinrich, and Marschke 2005, 328, 338; Anderson et al. 1991, 33, 37, and 39). As the GAO reported to Congress, "the need to meet performance levels may be the driving factor in deciding who receives WIA-funded services....Local staff are reluctant to provide WIA-funded services to job seekers who may be less likely to get and keep a job....As a result, individuals who are eligible for and may benefit from WIA-funded services may not be receiving services..." (GAO 2002, 14-15).

In any accountability system, no matter how carefully policy makers define subgroups, professionals who have direct contact with clients will always know more detail than policy makers about client characteristics and be able to game the system. In health care, Mark McClellan and his colleagues observed, "Doctors and hospitals likely have more detailed information about patients' health than the developer of a report card can, allowing them to choose to treat unobservably (to the analyst) healthier patients" (Dranove et al. 2003, 581). This is certainly true in schools, where teachers know more about their students' potential than administrators or policy makers can infer from prior test scores and a few demographic markers.

The private sector

When New York City Mayor Michael Bloomberg announced a 2007 teachers' union agreement to pay cash bonuses to teachers at schools where test scores increase, he said, "In the private sector, cash incentives are proven motivators for producing results. The most successful employees work harder, and everyone else tries to figure out how they can improve as well" (Gootman 2007). Eli Broad, whose foundation promotes incentive pay plans for teachers, added, "Virtually every other industry compensates employees based on how well they perform....We know from experience across other industries and sectors that linking performance and pay is a powerful incentive" (Bloomberg 2007).

These claims misrepresent how private sector firms motivate employees. Although incentive pay systems are commonplace, they are almost never based exclusively or even primarily on quantitative output measurement for professionals. Indeed, while the share of private sector workers who get performance pay has been increasing, the share who get such pay based on numerical output measures has been decreasing (see Adams and Heywood in this volume). The business management literature nowadays is filled with warnings about incentives that rely heavily on quantitative rather than qualitative measures.

For business organizations generally, quantitative performance measures are used warily, and never exclusively. Even stock prices or profit are not simple guides to public companies' performance and potential. The Securities and Exchange Commission has complex regulations designed to prevent publicly traded firms from using numerical indicators to mislead investors. Yet financial data are still too complex for laypersons to interpret—that is why investors rely on sophisticated analysts, employed to discern the underlying and often non-quantifiable potential that stock prices or other easily measured characteristics might obscure (Smith 1990, 70). Analysts sometimes disagree—equities markets exist only because quantitative indicators are not sufficiently transparent, and buyers and sellers have different interpretations of what firms' financial data mean.

SEC and private accounting standards are often defeated by an inability to control "creative accounting" to maximize bonuses. Among the most easily manipulated financial rules and business practices are depreciation schedules for long-term assets; accelerated or delayed shipments to or from inventories at the end of accounting periods; transfer of revenues or expenses between accounting periods; the allocation of overhead to inventories; and the expensing or capitalizing of major repair activities, research and development, or even advertising expenses (Healy 1985; Jaworski and Young 1992, 20; Smith 1990, 68; Schiff 1966). As with gaming in schools' test-based accountability systems, some but not all such manipulation is criminal. But before crossing that line, managers have considerable discretion (Jaworski and Young 1992, 20).

Most private sector jobs, as do teaching and other jobs in the public sector, include a composite of easily measured and less-easily measured responsibilities. Holding agents accountable only for the easily measured ones leads to goal distortion. Adding multiple measures of accountability is, by itself, insufficient to minimize such distortion.

Because of the ease with which most employees game purely quantitative incentives, most private sector accountability systems blend quantitative and qualitative measures, with most emphasis on the latter. This method characterizes accountability of relatively low- as well as high-level employees. McDonald's, for example, does not evaluate its store managers by sales volume or profitability alone. Instead, a manager and his or her supervisor establish targets for easily quantifiable measures such as sales volume and costs, but also for less easily quantifiable product quality, service, cleanliness, and personnel training, because these factors may affect long-term profitability as well as the reputation (and thus, profitability) of other outlets. Store managers are judged by the negotiated balance of these various factors (Kaplan and Atkinson 1998, 692-93). Wal-Mart uses a similar system. A like practice of negotiating qualitative as well as quantitative performance goals is also common for professionals in the private sector (Rothstein 2000).

Certainly, supervisory evaluation of employees is less reliable than numerical output measurements such as storewide sales or student test scores. Supervisory evaluation may be tainted by favoritism, bias, inflation and compression (narrowing the range of evaluations to avoid penalizing or rewarding too many employees), and even kickbacks or other forms of corruption (Ittner, Larcker, and Meyer 1997, 9).[7] Yet the widespread management use of subjective evaluations, despite these flaws, suggests that, as one personnel management review concludes, "It is better to imperfectly measure relevant dimensions than to perfectly measure irrelevant ones" (Bommer et al. 1995, 602). Or, "the prevalence of subjectivity in the performance measurement systems of virtually all [business] organizations suggests that exclusive reliance on distorted and risky objective measures is not an efficient alternative" (Baker 2002, 750).

Management of accountability systems in the private sector is labor intensive. Bain and Company, the management consulting firm, advises clients that judgment of results should always focus on long- and not short-term (and more easily quantifiable) goals. A company director estimated that, at Bain itself, each manager devotes about 100 hours a year to evaluating five employees for purposes of its incentive pay system. "When I try to imagine a school principal doing 30 reviews, I have trouble," he observed (Rothstein 2000).

A widespread business reform in recent decades has been "total quality management," promoted by W. Edwards Deming. He warned that businesses seeking to improve quality and thus long-term performance should eliminate work standards (quotas), eliminate management by numbers and numerical goals, and abolish merit ratings and "management by objective," because all of these encourage employees to focus on short-term results. "Management by numerical goal is an attempt to manage without knowledge of what to do, and in fact is usually management by fear," Deming insisted (Deming 1986, 76, 101-02).[8]

A corporate accountability tool that has grown in popularity is the balanced scorecard, first proposed in the early 1990s because business management theorists concluded that quantifiable short-term financial results were not accurate guides to future profitability. Firms' goals were too complex to be reduced to a few quantifiable measures, and future performance relies not only on a track record of financial success but on "intangible and intellectual assets, such as high quality products and services, motivated and skilled employees, responsive and predictable internal processes, and satisfied and loyal customers" (Kaplan and Atkinson 1998, 368). Management experts who promote the balanced scorecard approach to corporate accountability recommend that executives should supplement numerical output measures with judgments about the quality of organizational process, staff quality and morale, and customer satisfaction. Evaluation of a firm's performance, they say, should be "balanced between objective, easily quantifiable outcome measures and subjective, somewhat judgmental, performance drivers of the outcome measures" (Schick 2001, 50).

For "best-practice firms"[9] employing the balanced scorecard approach, the use "of subjective judgments reflects a belief that results-based compensation may not always be the ideal scheme for rewarding managers [because] many factors not under the control or influence of managers also affect reported performance [and] many managerial actions create (or destroy) economic value but may not be measured" (Kaplan and Norton 1996, 220).

Curiously, the federal government adopted a balanced scorecard approach simultaneously with its quantitative outcome-focused Government Performance Results Act and its test-based *No Child Left Behind Act*. Each year since 1988, the U.S. Department of Commerce has handed out Malcolm Baldrige National Quality Awards for exemplary institutions in manufacturing and other business sectors.[10] Numerical output indicators play only a small role in the department's award decisions: for the private sector, 450 out of 1,000 points are for "results" although, even here, results such as "ethical behavior," "social responsibility," "trust in senior leadership," "workforce capability and capacity," and "customer satisfaction and loyalty" are based on points awarded from qualitative judgments. Other criteria, also relying on qualitative evaluation, such as "how do senior leaders set organizational vision and values," and "protection of stakeholder and stockholder interests, as appropriate" make up the other 550 points (BNQP 2007a).

The Department of Commerce concluded that Baldrige principles of private sector quality could be applied as well to health and education institutions, so these were added to the reward system in 1999. For school districts, only 100 of 1,000 points are for "student learning outcomes," with other points awarded for subjectively evaluated measures such as "how senior leaders' personal actions reflect a commitment to the organization's values" (BNQP 2007b)

The most recent Baldrige award in elementary and secondary education was presented in 2005 to the Jenks (Oklahoma) school district. In making this award, the Department of Commerce cited the district's generally good test scores as well as its low teacher turnover and innovative programs such as an exchange relationship with schools in China and the enlistment of residents of a long-term care facility to mentor kindergartners and pre-kindergartners (BNQP 2007c). Yet the following year, the federal Department of Education deemed the Jenks district to be sub-standard according to NCLB rules, because Jenks' economically disadvantaged and special education students failed for two consecutive years to make "adequate yearly progress" in reading scores (Epperson 2007).

But no accountability at all is not the only alternative to the flawed approach of exclusive reliance on quantitative output measures. It is possible, indeed practical, to design an accountability system in education to ensure that schools and educators meet their responsibilities to deliver the broad range of outcomes that the American people demand, without relying exclusively on measures as imperfect as test scores. Such a system would be more expensive than our current regime of low-quality standardized tests, and would not give policy makers the comfortable, though false, precision that they want quantitative measures like test scores to provide.

These issue are discussed in great detail in a book I recently co-authored (with Rebecca Jacobsen and Tamara Wilder), *Grading Education: Getting Accountability Right*, which outlines the contours of a new accountability regime that is more responsive to these needs and outcomes. When NAEP was developed in the 1960s, its early design assessed a much broader range of outcomes than it does today. And throughout the nation, school accreditation teams provide the framework within which important elements of a balanced accountability system could be developed. Other nations have developed school inspection systems that illustrate such development. We discuss these issues in detail in our recent book (Rothstein et al. 2008) where we also outline the contours of a new accountability regime that is more responsive to these needs and outcomes.

Intrinsic motivation

In 1971, Edward Deci, a social psychologist, published results of experiments with college students. In his laboratory, experimental and control groups were observed playing a puzzle game. During the process, members of the experimental group were offered monetary rewards for solving the puzzles; later, the monetary rewards were withdrawn and both experimental and control groups continued to play. But the experimental group's performance declined after the monetary rewards were withdrawn.

Professor Deci replicated his laboratory experiment with a field experiment of similar design. He divided students who wrote headlines for a student newspaper into experimental and control groups; the experimental group received, for a limited period, monetary rewards for the speed with which they completed their assignments. Again, performance of the experimental writers fell behind that of the controls after monetary rewards ended.

Apparently, Professor Deci concluded, the students were initially intrinsically motivated to succeed in the game or headline writing, but the introduction of monetary rewards reduced this intrinsic motivation (Deci 1971). When they began to think of their goals as financial, they ceased caring as much about the intrinsic worth of the tasks.

Professor Deci did not examine the relevance of his findings to performance incentives for teachers or principals, but he did consider their implications for young children in school, examining the use of rewards (candy, extra recess, stars, tokens that can be exchanged for prizes) on student learning. Relying heavily on the work of educational psychologist Jerome Bruner, Deci concluded that such incentives may work well to improve classroom discipline. This is worthwhile, because it may not matter so much to a teacher what a child's reason for behaving might be, so long as the child behaves. And tokens may also improve test scores where only recall is involved. But "if one wishes to help children learn to think creatively, to develop lasting cognitive structure, and to be intrinsically motivated to learn, [such] reinforcement programs will interfere with these goals and therefore will be inappropriate" (Deci 1975, 219).[11]

Social psychologists continue to debate such conclusions. But the Deci experiments have also spawned research by management theorists to see if public service employees are more likely to be intrinsically motivated than private sector employees, and thus, whether monetary performance incentives might do harm to non-profit public sector professions in a way that might not occur in the private for-profit sector (Perry and Wise 1990; Pfeffer 1998, 116; Kreps 1997, 360; Courty, Heinrich, and Marschke 2005, 323; Gibbons 1998, 130).

In general, most management theorists conclude that public employees (including teachers) are relatively more motivated by a belief in the goals of their organizations, while private employees are relatively more motivated by financial rewards (Perry and Porter 1982, 94; Pearce, Stevenson, and Perry 1985, 262; Rainey 1982, 288). The General Social Survey (GSS), for example, finds that public sector employees are more likely to say that it is very important to them that a job be "helpful to society" and to "help others." Private sector employees are more likely to say that high pay, promotional opportunities, and job security are very important (Crewson 1997, 502-04). Even in a survey of the engineering profession, engineers working for the federal government were more likely to value making socially useful contributions while private sector engineers were more likely to value high income and promotions (Crewson 1997, 504-05). A survey of students entering management careers found that those entering the nonprofit and government sectors valued economic rewards less than those bound for the private sector.[12] A survey of middle managers in public and private enterprises found that the public managers gave less emphasis to financial career goals and greater emphasis to worthwhile social or public service (Rainey 1982). (School principals would be typical of such middle managers.) "Failure to properly understand and utilize the motivations of public employees may lead in the short term to poor job performance and in the long term to permanent displacement of a public service ethic," concludes a review of such surveys in a public administration journal (Crewson 1997, 500).

The differences between intrinsic and monetary incentives among public and private employees are not without limit. Some public sector or nonprofit employees are attracted to their agencies by job security, not idealism. Some private sector employees are attracted to their firms by the challenges and opportunities for creative satisfaction. Surveys of the intrinsic motivation literature in management and economics journals cite, for example, the zeal with which computer engineers at Data General rose to the challenge of developing a technologically advanced product, with long hours and at low pay, described by Tracy Kidder in his Pulitzer Prize–winning account, *The Soul of a New Machine.* (Perry and Wise 1990, 372; Kreps 1997, 362-63). (The book was published in 1982, long before days when payoffs to stock options became an inspiration to computer engineers.) But Tracy Kidder fans will also recall Chris Zajac, the Massachusetts schoolteacher-subject of Kidder's subsequent (1989) book, *Among Schoolchildren*, who traveled to Puerto Rico during spring vacation at her own expense, hoping to better understand the cultural assumptions about education that her students brought with them to school. It is unlikely that Mrs. Zajac would have done a more conscientious job as schoolteacher if she were offered monetary rewards for improved performance. Indeed, it is possible that such rewards may have been detrimental to her performance, if she became persuaded that efforts were not worth making if they were not rewarded financially. Mrs. Zajac's balance of financial and intrinsic motivations was perhaps more common among schoolteachers than was the balance of Data General engineers among business employees.

James Q. Wilson, in his study of bureaucracy, defined professionals as those "who receive some significant portion of their incentives from organized groups of fellow practitioners located outside the agency. Thus, the behavior of a professional in a bureaucracy is not wholly determined by incentives controlled by the agency" (Wilson 1989, 60). Although most experts investigating intrinsic motivation study managerial employees in federal and state bureaucracies, the considerations plausibly apply to teachers, many of whom enter the profession because of a belief in the mission of public education and a devotion to children, and whose loyalty is, in Wilson's terms, to the "norms" of the profession, not to their supervisors.

An important effort of school reform policy today is to increase the extent to which intrinsic rewards can motivate new teachers; the Teach for America program and the recruiting campaigns of many prominent charter schools (such as the KIPP academies) are illustrative.[13] The management literature suggests that performance incentive pay may work at cross-purposes with this effort.

The intrinsic rewards of teaching should not be exaggerated. As discrimination against women in the professions abates and female college graduates have a greater choice of professional careers, school districts face teacher shortages because compensation levels are too low to attract a sufficient supply, intrinsic rewards notwithstanding.

And it is possible, of course, that if the culture of public sector enterprises were transformed so that employees valued monetary rewards to a greater extent, and were less intrinsically motivated, performance would, on balance, improve. Perhaps institutional cultures are self-selecting, and public sector enterprises that re-oriented themselves around monetary incentives would attract different and more effective employees. But if the displaced intrinsic motivation is more powerful than monetary incentives in school teaching, shifting to pay-for-performance could have a net negative effect. Little research has been done to assess the likely risk or benefit of subverting teachers' intrinsic motivation with pay-for-performance.

Whether extrinsic rewards undermine professional norms is an ongoing subject of debate in health care, where the report cards issued by insurance companies have come increasingly to override doctors' professional judgment. A physician complains in a recent issue of *The New England Journal of Medicine* that he has "been marked down for not having an asthma plan for someone who no longer has asthma," and observes:

> U.S. doctors today have less and less to say about the care of their patients. All the complex lessons they learned in medical school are being swept aside for template care. Maybe I overestimate the next generation, but I can't imagine that young, creative people who are bright and talented enough to get into medical school will put up with this nonsense for very long. They aren't becoming physicians so they can fill in checklists and be told by a phone-bank operator what they can and cannot do for patients.

The author asks,

> Do we really want doctors who are motivated by wall plaques announcing their score on some "quality improvement" initiative? Will our enthusiasm for getting high grades, being declared superior to our colleagues, and earning performance bonuses overcome our profession's traditional capacity for critical thought and reliance on empirical data? (Vonnegut 2007)

Without these checklists, some patients with asthma did not have the proper treatment plan. This physician's complaint cannot itself settle whether the costs and benefits of substituting extrinsic for intrinsic motivation in medicine have been properly balanced.

2.3

Conclusion

That exclusively quantitative accountability systems result in goal distortion, gaming, and corruption in a wide variety of fields is not inconsistent with a conclusion that such systems nonetheless improve average performance in the narrow goals they measure. At the very least, they may direct attention to outliers that warrant further investigation. Several analyses by economists, management experts, and sociologists have concluded that narrowly quantitative incentive schemes have, at times, somewhat improved the average performance of medical care, job training, welfare, and private sector agents. The documentation of perverse consequences does not indicate that, in any particular case, the harm outweighed the benefits of such narrow quantitative accountability. The Soviet Union did, after all, industrialize from a feudal society in record time.

The survey, reported above, showing that physicians believe performance pay plans and the "shaming" publication of physician outcomes would result in avoidance of difficult cases and overlooking important but unmeasured aspects of treatment, also found that three-quarters of physicians continue to believe that pay-for-performance is beneficial overall. Accountability for waiting times for elective surgery in Great Britain did reduce average waiting times, notwithstanding some other perverse consequences.

One careful analysis of emergency room waiting times in Great Britain was unable to find evidence of perverse consequences expected from a narrow quantitative incentive. It could be, the authors conclude, "it is better to manage an organization using imperfect measures than using none at all." Performance incentive plans in medicine, both in the United States and Great Britain, did improve average outcomes in many respects, including cardiac surgery survival rates, the most frequently analyzed procedure (Kelman and Friedman 2007). And the General Accounting Office, while condemning the perverse incentives resulting from report cards in health care, nonetheless concluded, "We support the report card concept and encourage continued development in the field" (GAO 1994, 56).

In education, most policy makers who now promote performance incentives and accountability, and scholars who analyze them, seem mostly oblivious to the extensive literature in economics and management theory documenting the inevitable corruption of quantitative indicators and the perverse consequences of performance incentives that rely on such indicators. Of course, ignorant of this literature, many proponents of performance incentives in education are unable to engage in careful deliberation about whether, in particular cases, the benefits are worth the price.

How much gain in reading and math scores is necessary to offset the goal distortion—less art, music, physical education, science, history, character building—that inevitably results from rewarding teachers or schools for score gains only in math and reading? Will the gain in teacher quality from a performance incentive system be sufficient to justify the loss to the profession of intrinsic motivation as a driving force? How much misidentification of high- or low-performing teachers or schools is tolerable in order to improve the average performance of teachers or schools? How much curricular corruption, teaching to the test, are we willing to endure when we engage in "the folly of rewarding A while hoping for B" (Kerr 1975)?

These are difficult questions that proponents of performance incentives in education must answer. As yet, the questions have been mostly unasked.

Endnotes

1. See also citations in Darley (1991); Baker (2007); and Koretz (2007).

2. There is also the possibility that non-random allocation of teachers to classrooms (by principals or others) will affect their value-added—Rothstein (2009) finds evidence of such allocation of teachers for schools in North Carolina.

3. The term "input" is often used in education policy discussion to refer only to school resources, such as teachers, class sizes, textbooks, etc. This definition is too limited. If the outcome, or dependent variable, is student achievement, then the inputs, or independent variables, include not only resources but also students with their varied characteristics.

4. This book is not the first, or only, discussion of the applicability of Campbell's law to contemporary test-based educational accountability policies. Nichols and Berliner (2007) and Koretz (2007; 2008) have made similar observations.

5. Citations in text omitted.

6. In congressional testimony regarding TANF reauthorization in 2005, Assistant Secretary of Health and Human Services Wade Horn proposed that the performance incentive program be cut in half, and used only to reward employment outcomes (Horn 2005). However, even this reduced program was not implemented

7. That labor market success seems to be correlated with employees' physical attractiveness confirms that supervisory evaluations are flawed tools for objective evaluations of performance. See Hamermesh and Biddle (1994).

8.   See also Pfeffer (1998) and Deming Institute (2007). Deming was not hostile to quantitative analysis where he thought it appropriate. He advocated analysis of factors that contribute to quality and performance through statistical modeling.

9.   The influential work (Kaplan and Norton 1996) describing the balanced scorecard approach relies on descriptions of illustrative firms, including Rockwater (an undersea construction company that is a division of Brown and Root, now a subsidiary of Haliburton), Analog Devices, FMC Corporation, and five pseudonymous firms in the banking, retail, petroleum, and insurance industries. Other balanced scorecard case studies are included in Kaplan and Atkinson (1998) pp. 380-441.

10.   For a discussion, see Stecher and Kirby (2004).

11.   Widespread contemporary enthusiasm for performance incentives in education finds dramatic expression in New York City's new experiment to pay substantial cash rewards to low-income students for high test scores. See Medina (2007).

12.   Cited in Perry and Porter (1982), p. 90.

13.   Teach for America and similar efforts initially attempted to attract the most academically talented college graduates into teaching with recruiting drives at Ivy League and other elite colleges. These recruits were not likely to have entered teaching without the idealistic appeal of the recruitment effort. But as these programs have expanded, they have recruited deeper in the talent pool. Chris Zajac, of Tracy Kidder's account, was more typical of the nation's schoolteachers: the daughter of a factory worker, she taught in the Irish working-class community where she was raised.

Bibliography

(In each case where an Internet address (URL) is given, the citation was accessed and rechecked on August 15, 2008 to confirm its accuracy as of that date. In cases where URLs given are no longer valid, readers are invited to contact the author to obtain a copy of the document.)

Altman, Lawrence K. 1990. Heart-surgery death rates decline in New York. *New York Times,* December 5.

Anderson, Kathryn H., Richard V. Burkhauser, Jennie E. Raymond, and Clifford S. Russell. 1991. Mixed signals in the Job Training Partnership Act. *Growth & Change.* Vol. 22(3), pp. 32-48.

Associated Press. 1993. Rating of hospitals is delayed on ground of flaws in data." *New York Times*, June 23.

Baker, George. 2002. Distortion and risk in optimal performance contracts. *Journal of Human Resources.* Vol. 37(4), pp. 728-51.

Baker, George. 2007. "Performance indicators, distortion, and Campbell's Law of Good Intentions." (Powerpoint). Prepared for the Eric M. Mindich Conference on Experimental Social Science: Biases from Behavioral Responses to Measurement: Perspectives from Theoretical Economics, Health Care, Education, and Social Services. Cambridge, Massachusetts, May 4.

Barnow, Burt S., and Jeffrey A. Smith. 2004. Performance management of U.S. job training programs: Lessons from the Job Training Partnership Act. *Public Finance & Management.* Vol. 4(3), pp. 247-87.

Bevan, Gwyn, and Christopher Hood. 2006. What's measured Is what matters: Targets and gaming in the English public health care system. *Public Administration.* Vol. 84(3), 517-38.

Bird, Sheila M., Sir David Cox, Vern T. Farewell, Harvey Goldstein, Tim Holt, and Peter C. Smith. 2005. Performance indicators: Good, bad, and ugly. *Journal of the Royal Statistical Society.* Series A, Vol. 168(1) pp. 1-27.

Blalock, Ann, and Burt Barnow. 2001. "Is the New Obsession With 'Performance Management' Masking the Truth About Social Programs?" In Dall W. Forsythe, ed., *Quicker, Better, Cheaper: Managing Performance in American Government.* Albany, N.Y.: Rockefeller Institute Press.

Blau, Peter Michael. 1955 (rev. 1963). *The Dynamics of Bureaucracy; A Study of Interpersonal Relations in Two Government Agencies.* Chicago, Ill.: University of Chicago Press.

Bloomberg, Michael. 2007. "Mayor's Press Release." No. 375, New York, N.Y. October 17.

BNQP (Baldrige National Quality Program). 2007a. "Criteria for Performance Excellence." Washington, D.C.: Baldrige National Quality Program, National Institute of Standards and Technology, Technology Administration, U.S. Department of Commerce. http://www.quality.nist.gov/ PDF_files/2007_Business_Nonprofit_Criteria.pdf

BNQP (Baldrige National Quality Program). 2007b. "Education Criteria for Performance Excellence." Washington, D.C.: Baldrige National Quality Program, National Institute of Standards and Technology, Technology Administration, U.S. Department of Commerce. http://www. quality.nist.gov/PDF_files/2007_Education_Criteria.pdf.

BNQP (Baldrige National Quality Program). 2007c. "2005 Award Winner." Washington, D.C.: Baldrige National Quality Program, National Institute of Standards and Technology, Technology Administration, U.S. Department of Commerce. http://www.quality.nist.gov/PDF_files/Jenks_ Public_Schools_Profile.pdf

Bommer, William H., Jonathan L. Johnson, Gregory A. Rich, Philip M. Podsakoff, and Scott B. McKenzie. 1995. On the interchangeability of objective and subjective measures of employee performance: A meta-analysis. *Personnel Psychology*. Vol. 48(3), pp. 587-605.

Campbell, Donald T. 1979. Assessing the impact of planned social change. *Evaluation and Program Planning*. Vol 2, pp. 67-90. (Reprinted, with minor revisions and additions, from Gene M. Lyons, ed., 1975. *Social Research and Public Policies*. Hanover, N.H.: University Press of New England.)

Carnoy, Martin, Rebecca Jacobsen, Lawrence Mishel, and Richard Rothstein. 2005. *The Charter School Dust-Up. Examining the Evidence on Enrollment and Achievement*. Washington, D.C.: Economic Policy Institute.

Casalino, Lawrence P., G. Caleb Alexander, Lei Jin, and R. Tamara Konetzka. 2007. General internists' views on pay-for-performance and public reporting of quality scores: A national survey. *Health Affairs*. Vol. 26(2), pp. 492-99.

Courty, Pascal, Carolyn Heinrich, and Gerald Marschke. 2005. Setting the standard in performance measurement systems. *International Public Management Journal*. Vol. 8(3), pp 321-47.

Courty, Pascal, and Gerald Marschke. 1997. Measuring government performance: Lessons from a federal job-training program. *American Economic Review*. Vol 87(2), 383-88.

Crewson, Philip E. 1997. Public-service motivation: Building empirical evidence of incidence and effect. *Journal of Public Administration Research and Theory*. Vol. 7(4), pp. 499-518.

Darley, John. 1991. Setting standards seeks control, risks distortions. *Institute of Governmental Studies Public Affairs Report*. Vol. 32(4).

Deci, Edward L. 1971. Effects of externally mediated rewards on intrinsic motivation. *Journal of Personality and Social Psychology*. Vol.18 (1), pp. 105-115, April.

Deci, Edward L. 1975. *Intrinsic Motivation*. New York: Plenum Press.

Deming, W. Edwards. 1986. *Out of the Crisis*. Cambridge: Massachusetts Institute of Technology, Center for Advanced Engineering Study.

Deming Institute (The W. Edwards Deming Institute). 2007. "Teachings." Palos Verdes Estates, Calif.: Deming Institute. http://deming.org/index.cfm?content=66

Dranove, David, Daniel Kessler, Mark McClellan, and Mark Satterthwaite. 2003. Is more information better? The effects of report cards' on health care providers. *Journal of Political Economy*. 111(3), pp. 555-88.

Epperson, Shaun. 2007. Jenks School misses NCLB standard. *Tulsa World*. November 14.

Epstein, Arnold. 1995. Performance reports on quality—prototypes, problems, and prospects. *New England Journal of Medicine*. Vol. 333(1), pp. 57-61.

Farhi, Paul. 1996. Television 'sweeps' stakes. *Washington Post*, November 17.

Finder, Alan. 2007. College ratings race roars on despite concerns. *New York Times*, August 17.

GAO (U. S. General Accounting Office). 1994. *Health Care Reform. "Report Cards" Are Useful but Significant Issues Need to Be Addressed*. Washington, D.C.: General Accounting Office, September.

GAO (U. S. General Accounting Office). 2002. *Workforce Investment Act: Improvements Needed in Performance Measures to Provide a More Accurate Picture of WIA's Effectiveness*. Washington, D.C.: General Accounting Office. February.

Gibbons, Robert. 1998. Incentives in organizations. *The Journal of Economic Perspectives*. Vol. 12 (4), Autumn, pp. 115-32.

Goddard, Maria, Russell Mannion, and Peter C. Smith. 2000. "The Performance Framework: Taking Account of Economic Behaviour." In P.C. Smith, ed., *Reforming Markets in Health Care*. Buckingham, England: Open University Press.

Goodlad, John I. 1984 (2004 edition). *A Place Called School*. McGraw Hill.

Gootman, Elissa. 2007. Teachers agree to bonus pay tied to scores. *New York Times*, October 18.

Green, Jesse, Leigh J. Passman, and Neil Wintfeld. 1991. Analyzing hospital mortality: The consequences of diversity in patient mix. *Journal of the American Medical Association*. Vol. 265, pp. 1849-53.

Green, Jesse, and Neil Wintfeld. 1995. Report cards on Cardiac surgeons: Assessing New York state's approach. *New England Journal of Medicine*. Vol. 332(18), pp. 1229-33.

Hamermesh, Daniel S., and Jeff E. Biddle. 1994. Beauty and the labor market. *American Economic Review*. Vol. 84, pp. 1174-94.

Harris, Gardiner. 2007. Report rates hospitals on their heart treatment. *New York Times,* June 22.

Healy, Paul M. 1985. The effect of bonus schemes on accounting decisions. *Journal of Accounting and Economics.* Vol. 7, pp. 85-107.

Heckman, James J., Carolyn Heinrich, and Jeffrey Smith. 2002. The performance of performance standards. *Journal of Human Resources.* Vol. 37, No. 4, pp. 778-811.

Heinrich, Carolyn J. 2004. Improving public-Sector performance management: One step forward, two steps back? *Public Finance and Management.* Vol. 4, No. 3, pp. 317-51.

Heinrich, Carolyn J., and Youseok Choi. 2007. Performance-based contracting in social welfare programs. *American Review of Public Administration.* Vol. 37, No. 4, pp. 409-35.

Heinrich, Carolyn J., and Gerald Marschke. 2007. "Dynamics in performance measurement system design and implementation." July (draft).

Horn, Wade F. 2005. "Welfare reform reauthorization proposals." Testimony before the Subcommittee on Human Resources, House Ways and Means Committee, February 10. http://www.acf. dhhs.gov/programs/olab/legislative/testimony/2005/welfare_reform_testimony.html

Hoyt, Clark. 2007. Books for the ages, if not for the best-seller list. *New York Times,* October 21.

Iezzoni, Lisa I. 1994. "Risk and Outcomes." In Lisa I. Iezzoni, ed., *Risk Adjustment for Measuring Health Care Outcomes.* Ann Arbor, Mich.: Health Administration Press.

Iezzoni, Lisa I., Michael Shwartz, Arlene S. Ash, John S. Hughes, Jennifer Daley, and Yevgenia D. Mackiernan. 1995. Using severity-adjusted stroke mortality rates to judge hospitals. *International Journal for Quality in Health Care.* Vol. 7, No. 2, pp. 81-94.

Ittner, Christopher D., David F. Larcker, and Marshall W. Meyer. 1997. *Performance, Compensation, and the Balanced Scorecard.* Philadelphia: Wharton School, University of Pennsylvania, November 1. http://knowledge.wharton.upenn.edu/papers/405.pdf

Jackman, Tom. 2004. Falls Church police must meet quota for tickets. *Washington Post,* August 8.

Jaschik, Scott. 2007. Should U.S. news make presidents rich? *Inside Higher Ed.* (Insidehighered. com). March 19. http://www.insidehighered.com/news/2007/03/19/usnews

Jaworski, Bernard J., and S. Mark Young. 1992. Dysfunctional behavior and management control: An empirical study of marketing managers. *Accounting, Organizations, and Society.* Vol. 17(1), pp. 17-35.

Johnson, Ryan M., David H. Reiley, and Juan Carlos Munoz. 2006. "'The war for the fare.' How driver compensation affects bus system performance." August (draft). http://www.u.arizona. edu/~dreiley/papers/WarForTheFare.pdf

Kaplan, Robert S., and Anthony A. Atkinson. 1998. *Advanced Management Accounting.* Third Edition. Englewood Cliffs, N.J.: Prentice Hall.

Kaplan, Robert S., and David P. Norton. 1996. *The Balanced Scorecard: Translating Strategy Into Action.* Boston, Mass.: Harvard Business School Press.

Kassirer, Jerome P. 1994. The use and abuse of practice profiles. *New England Journal of Medicine.* Vol. 330(9), pp. 634-36.

Kelman, Steven, and John N. Friedman. 2007. "Performance improvement and performance dysfunction: An empirical examination of impacts of the emergency room wait-time target in the English National Health Service." Faculty Research Working Paper No. RWP07-034. Cambridge, Mass.: Kennedy School of Government, August.

Kerr, Steven. 1975. On the folly of rewarding A while hoping for B. *Academy of Management Journal.* Vol. 18(4), pp. 769-83.

Kidder, Tracy. 1989. *Among Schoolchildren.* Boston, Mass.: Houghton Mifflin.

Koretz, Daniel. 2007. "Inflation of scores in educational accountability systems: Empirical findings and a psychometric framework." Powerpoint presentation prepared for the Eric M. Mindich Conference on Experimental Social Science: Biases From Behavioral Responses to Measurement: Perspectives From Theoretical Economics, Health Care, Education, and Social Services. Cambridge, Mass., May 4.

Koretz, Daniel M. 2008. *Measuring Up: What Educational Testing Really Tells Us.* Cambridge, Mass.: Harvard University Press.

Kreps, David M. 1997. Intrinsic motivation and extrinsic incentives. *The American Economic Review.* Vol. 87(2), pp. 359-364, May.

Ladd, Helen F. 2007. "Holding schools accountable revisited." 2007 Spencer Foundation Lecture in Education Policy and Management, Association for Public Policy Analysis and Management. http://www.appam.org/awards/pdf/2007Spencer-Ladd.pdf

Ladd, Helen F., and Arnaldo Zelli. 2002. School-based accountability in North Carolina: The responses of school principals. *Educational Administration Quarterly.* Vol. 38(4), pp. 494-529.

Lapointe, Archie E., and Stephen L. Koffler. 1982. Your standards or mine? The case for the National Assessment of Educational Progress. *Educational Researcher.* Vol. 11(10), pp. 4-11.

Lee, Jaekyung. 2006. *Tracking Achievement Gaps and Assessing the Impact of NCLB on the Gaps: An In-Depth Look Into National and State Reading and Math Outcome Trends.* Cambridge, Mass.: Civil Rights Project at Harvard University. http://www.civilrightsproject.ucla.edu/ research/esea/nclb_naep_lee.pdf

Levy, Frank, and Peter Temin. 2007. "Inequality and institutions in 20th century America." Working Paper No. W13106. Cambridge, Mass.: National Bureau of Economic Research.

Linn, Robert L. 2000. Assessments and accountability. *Educational Researcher*. Vol. 29(2), pp. 4-16.

Linn, Robert L. 2006. *Educational Accountability Systems*. CSE Technical Report 687. Los Angeles, Calif.: National Center for Research on Evaluation, Standards, and Student Testing, June.

Liu, Goodwin. 2006. Interstate inequality in educational opportunity. *New York University Law Review*. Vol. 81(6), pp. 2044-128.

Liu, Goodwin. 2008. Improving Title I funding equity across states, districts, and schools. *Iowa Law Review*. Vol. 93, pp. 973-1013.

Livingston, Samuel A., and Michael J. Zieky. 1982. *Passing Scores: A Manual for Setting Standards of Performance on Educational and Occupational Tests*. Princeton, N.J.: Educational Testing Service.

Loomis, Susan Cooper, and Mary Lyn Bourque, eds. 2001a. *National Assessment of Educational Progress Achievement Levels, 1992-1998 for Mathematics*. Washington, D.C.: National Assessment Governing Board, July. http://www.nagb.org/pubs/mathbook.pdf

Loomis, Susan Cooper, and Mary Lyn Bourque, eds. 2001b. *National Assessment of Educational Progress Achievement Levels, 1992-1998 for Writing*. Washington, D.C.: National Assessment Governing Board. July. http://www.nagb.org/pubs/writingbook.pdf

Lu, Susan Feng. 2007. *Multitasking, Information Disclosure, and Product Quality: Evidence From Nursing Homes*. Chicago, Ill.: Kellogg School of Management, Northwestern University, November 15. http://www.kellogg.northwestern.edu/faculty/lu/multitasking.pdf

McKee, Martin. 1996. "Discussion of the paper by Goldstein and Spiegelhalter." In Harvey Goldstein and David J. Spiegelhalter. *League Tables and Their Limitations: Statistical Issues in Comparisons of Institutional Performance* (with discussion)." *Journal of the Royal Statistical Society*. Series A 159, pp. 385-443.

McKee, Martin, and Duncan Hunter. 1994. "What Can Comparisons of Hospital Death Rates Tell Us About the Quality of Care?" In T. Delamothe, ed., *Outcomes Into Clinical Practice*. London: British Medical Journal Press.

Medina, Jennifer. 2007. His charge: Find a key to students' success. *The New York Times*, June 21.

Moore, Solomon. 2007. In California, deputies held competition on arrests. *New York Times*, October 5.

Morrissey, W. R. 1972. Nixon anti-crime plan undermines crime statistics. *Justice Magazine*. Vol. 5/6, pp. 8-14.

Mullen, P.M. 1985. Performance indicators: Is anything new? *Hospital and Health Services Review*. pp. 165-67, July.

Murray, Michael. 2005. Why arrest quotas are wrong. *PBA Magazine*. Spring. http://www. nycpba.org/publications/mag-05-spring/murray.html

Nichols, Sharon L., and David C. Berliner. 2007. *Collateral Damage: How High-Stakes Testing Corrupts America's Schools*. Cambridge, Mass.: Harvard Education Press.

Nove, A. 1964. "Economic Irrationality and Irrational Statistics." Chapter 16 in A. Nove, ed., *Economic Rationality and Soviet Politics; or, Was Stalin Really Necessary?* London: George Allen & Unwin.

Pearce, Jone L., William B. Stevenson, and James L. Perry. 1985. Managerial compensation based on organizational performance: A time series analysis of the effects of merit pay. *Academy of Management Journal*. Vol. 28(2), pp. 261-78, June.

Perry, James L., and Lyman W. Porter. 1982. Factors affecting the context for motivation in public organizations. *The Academy of Management Review*. Vol. 7(1), pp. 89-98, January.

Perry, James L., and Lois Recascino Wise. 1990. The motivational bases of public service. *Public Administration Review*. Vol. 50(3), 367-73, May/June.

Pfeffer, Jeffrey. 1998. Six dangerous myths about pay. *Harvard Business Review*. Vol. 76, No.3, pp. 108-19.

Rainey, Hal G. 1982. Reward preferences among public and private managers: In search of the service ethic. *The American Review of Public Administration*. Vol. 16(4), pp. 288-302, December.

Ridley, Clarence E., and Herbert A. Simon. 1938, 1943. *Measuring Municipal Activities: A Survey of Suggested Criteria for Appraising Administration*. Chicago, Ill.: International City Managers' Association.

Rothstein, Richard. 2000. Making a case against performance pay. *New York Times*, April 26.

Rothstein, Jesse. 2009 (Forthcoming). Student sorting and bias in value added estimation: Selection on observables and unobservables. *Education Finance and Policy*.

Rothstein, Richard, Rebecca Jacobson, and Tamara Wilder. 2008. *Grading Education:Getting Accountability Right*. Washington, D.C.: Economic Policy Institute.

Santora, Marc. 2005. Cardiologists say rankings sway choices on surgery. *New York Times*, January 11.

Schick, Allen. 2001. "Getting Performance Measures to Measure Up." In D.W. Forsythe, ed., *Quicker, Better, Cheaper: Managing Performance in American Government*. Albany, N.Y.: Rockefeller Institute Press.

Schiff, Michael. 1966. Accounting tactics and the theory of the firm. *Journal of Accounting Research*. Vol. 4(1), 62-67.

Seidman, David, and Michael Couzens. 1974. Getting the crime rate down: Political pressure and crime reporting. *Law & Society Review*. Vol. 8(3), pp. 457-94.

Simon, Herbert A. 1978. "Rational decision-making in business organizations." Nobel Memorial Lecture, December 8. http://nobelprize.org/nobel_prizes/economics/laureates/1978/simon-lecture.pdf

Skolnick, Jerome H. 1966. *Justice Without Trial: Law Enforcement in Democratic Society*. New York, N.Y.: Wiley.

Smith, Peter. 1990. The use of performance indicators in the public sector. *Journal of the Royal Statistical Society*. Series A 153, pp. 53-72.

Smith, Peter. 1993. Outcome-related performance indicators and organizational control in the public sector. *British Journal of Management*. Vol. 4(3), pp. 135-51.

Smith, Peter. 1995. On the unintended consequences of publishing performance data in the public sector. *International Journal of Public Administration*. Vol. 18(2 & 3), pp. 277-310.

Stecher, Brian, and Sheila Nataraj Kirby, eds. 2004. *Organizational Improvement and Accountability: Lessons for Education From Other Sectors*. Santa Monica, Calif.: RAND. http://www.rand.org/pubs/monographs/2004/RAND_MG136.pdf

Steinbrook, Robert. 2006. Public report cards: Cardiac surgery and beyond. *New England Journal of Medicine*. Vol. 355(18), pp. 1847-49.

Timmins, Nicholas. 2005. Blair bemused over gp waiting times. *Financial Times*, April 30.

Twigg, R. 1972. Downgrading of crimes verified in Baltimore. *Justice Magazine*. Vol.5(6), pp. 1, 15-18.

Uhlig, Mark A. 1987. Transit police remove officer for quota plan. *New York Times,* December 21.

Vonnegut, Mark. 2007. Is quality improvement improving quality? A view from the doctor's office." *The New England Journal of Medicine.* Vol. 327(26), pp. 2652-53, December.

West, Martin. 2007. "Testing, Learning, and Teaching: The Effects of Test-Based Accountability on Student Achievement and Instructional Time in Core Academic Subjects." In Chester E. Finn Jr., and Diane Ravitch, eds., *Beyond the Basics: Achieving a Liberal Education for All Children*. Washington, D.C.: Thomas B. Fordham Institute, pp. 45-62.

Wilson, James Q. 1989. *Bureaucracy: What Government Agencies Do and Why They Do It*. New York, N.Y.: Basic Books.

Wiseman, Michael. 2007. "Performing for prizes: The high performance bonus as an instrument for improving management of American social assistance." Paper presented at the Ninth Public Management Research Conference, Public Management Research Association, Tucson, Ariz., October 25-27.

ACKNOWLEDGEMENTS

EPI appreciates the Ford Foundation—and Fred Frelow in particular—for supporting the research in the Economic Policy Institute's Series on Alternative Teacher Compensation Systems.

All of the authors of this volume want to express their gratitude to the Economic Policy Institute's publications staff—department director Joseph Procopio, editor Ellen Levy, and designer Sylvia Saab—for their dedication and hard work in the launching of this new EPI book series.

PART I: PERFORMANCE PAY IN THE U.S. PRIVATE SECTOR

The authors thank Daniel Parent for his helpful conversations and for sharing his estimates from the PSID. They also thank Patrick O'Halloran for assistance with the NLSY97. Anthony Barkume and Al Schenk deserve thanks for their efforts in explaining the BLS Employment Cost Index and for preparing several special tabulations used in this report. We acknowledge that those special tabulations have not passed the usual BLS procedures for guaranteeing quality and reliability. Heywood thanks both Michelle Brown and Uwe Jirjahn for histories of fruitful joint work on performance pay. Both authors also thank the readers of various drafts of their study, particularly Matt Wiswall, Marigee Bacolod, and Jason Faberman for their helpful reviews. None of those mentioned are responsible for the results or opinions expressed here.

PART II: THE PERILS OF QUANTITATIVE PERFORMANCE ACCOUNTABILITY

Part of this study was prepared for presentation at the conference, "Performance Incentives: Their Growing Impact on American K-12 Education," sponsored by the National Center on Performance Incentives at Peabody College, Vanderbilt University, February 27-29, 2008. Support for this research was also provided by the Campaign for Educational Equity, Teachers College, Columbia University. The views expressed in this chapter are those of the author alone, and do not necessarily represent the views of the Economic Policy Institute, the Campaign for Educational Equity, Teachers College, Columbia University, or the National Center on Performance Incentives, Peabody College, or Vanderbilt University.

I am heavily indebted to Daniel Koretz, who has been concerned for many years with how "high stakes" can render test results unrepresentative of the achievement they purport to measure, and who noticed long ago that similar problems arose in other fields. Discussions with Professor Koretz, as I embarked on this project, were invaluable. I am also indebted to Professor Koretz for sharing his file of newspaper clippings on this topic and for inviting me to attend a seminar he organized, the "Eric M. Mindich Conference on Experimental Social Science: Biases from Behavioral Responses to Measurement: Perspectives from Theoretical Economics, Health Care, Education, and Social Services," in Cambridge, Massachusetts, May 4, 2007. Several participants in that seminar, particularly George Baker of the Harvard Business School, Carolyn Heinrich of the Lafollette School of Public Affairs at the University of Wisconsin, and Meredith Rosenthal of the Harvard School of Public Health were generous in introducing me to the literatures in their respective fields, answering my follow-up questions, and referring me to other experts. Much of this chapter results from following sources initially identified by these experts.

Access to literature from many academic and policy fields, within and outside education, was enhanced with extraordinary help of Janet Pierce and her fellow-librarians at the Gottesman Libraries of Teachers College, Columbia University.

Others have previously surveyed this field. Stecher and Kirby (2004), like the present effort, did so to gain insights relating to public education. But their survey has attracted insufficient attention in discussions of education accountability, so another effort is called for. Haney and Raczek (1994), in a paper for the U.S. Office of Technology Assessment, warned of problems similar to those analyzed here that would arise if quantitative accountability systems were developed for education. Two surveys, Kelman and Friedman (2007), and Adams and Heywood (this volume) were published or became available to me while I was researching this chapter and summarized some of the same issues in a fashion which this chapter, in many respects, duplicates. Susan Moore Johnson reminded me about debates in the early 1980s about whether teachers' intrinsic motivation might be undermined by an extrinsic reward-for-performance system.

A forthcoming Columbia University Ph.D. dissertation in sociology, contrasting "risk adjustment" in medical accountability systems with the absence of such adjustment in school accountability, should make an important contribution (Booher-Jennings, forthcoming).

This chapter cites studies from the business, management, health, and human capital literatures, as well as previous surveys of those literatures, in particular Baker (1992), Holmstrom and Milgrom (1991), Mullen (1985), and Blalock and Barnow (2001). I am hopeful, however, that this chapter organizes the evidence in a way that may be uniquely useful to education policy makers grappling with problems of performance incentives in education.

This chapter has benefited from criticisms and suggestions of readers of a preliminary draft. I am solely responsible for remaining errors and misinterpretations, including those that result from my failure to follow these readers' advice. For very helpful suggestions, I am grateful to Marcia Angell, Julie Berry Cullen, Carolyn Heinrich, Jeffrey Henig, Rebecca Jacobsen, Trent Kaufman, Ellen Condliffe Lagemann, Lawrence Mishel, Howard Nelson, Bella Rosenberg, Joydeep Roy, Brian Stecher, and Tamara Wilder.

About the Authors

SCOTT J. ADAMS is Associate Professor of Economics and faculty member in the Graduate Program in Human Resources and Labor Relations at the University of Wisconsin-Milwaukee. He has previously worked as a Robert Wood Johnson Fellow in Health Policy Research at the University of Michigan. He worked at the President's Council of Economic Advisers as senior economist responsible for education and labor. His research on labor issues has been published in the *Journal of Human Resources*, *Journal of Public Economics*, *Economics of Education Review*, and the *Journal of Urban Economics*.

JOHN S. HEYWOOD is Distinguished Professor of Economics and Director of the Graduate Program in Human Resources and Labor Relations at the University of Wisconsin-Milwaukee. He holds a concurrent position with the School of Business at the University of Birmingham in the United Kingdom. His research on performance pay has been widely published including in the *Journal of Political Economy*, *Journal of Human Resources,* and *Economica*. He also co-edited the recent text *Paying for Performance: An International Comparison.*

RICHARD ROTHSTEIN is a research associate of the Economic Policy Institute. From 1999 to 2002 he was the national education columnist of *The New York Times*. He was a member of the national task force that drafted the statement, "A Broader, Bolder Approach to Education" (www.boldapproach.org). He is also the author of *Class and Schools: Using Social, Economic, and Educational Reform to Close the Black-White Achievement Gap* (EPI & Teachers College 2004) and *The Way We Were? Myths and Realities of America's Student Achievement* (1998). Rothstein was a co-author of the books *The Charter School Dust-Up: Examining the Evidence on Enrollment and Achievement* (2005) and *All Else Equal: Are Public and Private Schools Different?* (2003). A full listing of Rothstein's publications on education and other economic policy issues, including links, can be found at www.epi.org/author_publications.cfm?author_id=271. He can be contacted at riroth@epi.org.

About EPI

THE ECONOMIC POLICY INSTITUTE was founded in 1986 to widen the debate about policies to achieve healthy economic growth, prosperity, and opportunity. Today, despite rapid growth in the U.S. economy in the latter part of the 1990s, inequality in wealth, wages, and income remains historically high. Expanding global competition, changes in the nature of work, and rapid technological advances are altering economic reality. Yet many of our policies, attitudes, and institutions are based on assumptions that no longer reflect real world conditions.

With the support of leaders from labor, business, and the foundation world, the Institute has sponsored research and public discussion of a wide variety of topics: globalization; fiscal policy; trends in wages, incomes, and prices; education; the causes of the productivity slowdown; labor market problems; rural and urban policies; inflation; state-level economic development strategies; comparative international economic performance; and studies of the overall health of the U.S. manufacturing sector and of specific key industries.

The Institute works with a growing network of innovative economists and other social-science researchers in universities and research centers all over the country who are willing to go beyond the conventional wisdom in considering strategies for public policy. Founding scholars of the Institute include Jeff Faux, former EPI president; Lester Thurow, Sloan School of Management, MIT; Ray Marshall, former U.S. secretary of labor, professor at the LBJ School of Public Affairs, University of Texas; Barry Bluestone, Northeastern University; Robert Reich, former U.S. secretary of labor; and Robert Kuttner, author, editor of *The American Prospect*, and columnist for *Business Week* and the *Washington Post* Writers Group.

For additional information about the Institute, contact EPI at 1333 H St. NW, Suite 300, Washington, D.C. 20005, (202) 775-8810, or visit www.epi.org.

OTHER BOOKS FROM
THE ECONOMIC POLICY INSTITUTE

THE STATE OF WORKING AMERICA 2008/2009
by Lawrence Mishel, Jared Bernstein, and Heidi Shierholz

Prepared biennially since 1988, EPI's flagship publication sums up the problems and challenges facing American working families, presenting a wide variety of data on family incomes, taxes, wages, unemployment, wealth, and poverty—data that enables the book's authors to closely examine the impact of the economy on the living standards of the American people. *The State of Working America 2008/2009* is an exhaustive reference work that will be welcomed by anyone eager for a comprehensive portrait of the economic well-being of the nation.

From Cornell University Press, January 2009. For more information, visit StateofWorkingAmerica.org.

ISBN: 1-932066-34-9(paperback) $ 24.95, ISBN: 1-932066-35-7(cloth) $ 59.95

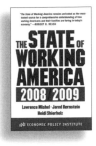

GRADING EDUCATION
GETTING ACCOUNTABILITY RIGHT
by Richard Rothstein, Rebecca Jacobsen, Tamara Wilder

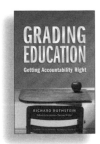

Accountability policies like No Child Left Behind, based exclusively on math and reading test scores, have narrowed the curriculum, misidentified school performance, and established irresponsible expectations. Instead of just grading progress in one or two narrow subjects, we should hold schools accountable for the broad outcomes we expect from public education—basic knowledge and skills, critical thinking, an appreciation of the arts, physical and emotional health, and preparation for skilled employment—and then develop the means to measure, and ensure, schools' success in achieving them. This book describes a new kind of accountability plan for public education. It relies upon both higher quality testing and professional evaluation.

Published by the Economic Policy Institute and Teachers College Press.

ISBN-10: 0-8077-4939-5, ISBN-13: 978-0-8077-4939-5, 6" x 9", paper, 280 pages, October 2008, $19.95

THE CASE FOR COLLABORATIVE SCHOOL REFORM
THE TOLEDO EXPERIENCE
by Ray Marshall

The Case for Collaborative School Reform argues that the most successful school reforms will be undertaken collaboratively between teachers, school district officials, and union leaders. The study focuses on the superior results of the reform efforts of the Toledo School District and the Toledo Federation of Teachers, an innovative and collaborative teachers union In a representative urban school district. Toledo's experience not only demonstrates the value of union-management collaboration to focus the parties' attention and efforts on school reform, but also illustrates the evolution of school policies toward a greater focus on student achievement.

ISBN: 1-93-2066-31-4, 6" x 9", paper, 112 pages, July 2008, $13.50

THE TEACHING PENALTY
TEACHER PAY LOSING GROUND
by Sylvia Allegretto, Sean P. Corcoran, and Lawrence Mishel

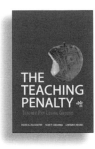

For decades, researchers have asked whether teacher compensation has kept pace without side job opportunities, and whether compensation is sufficiently competitive to attract the quality of instructors desired. While the popular view is that teacher pay is relatively low and has not kept up with comparable professions over time, new claims suggest that teachers are actually well compensated when work hours, weeks of work, or benefits packages are taken into account.

The Teaching Penalty reviews recent analyses of relative teacher compensation and provides a detailed analysis of trends in the relative weekly pay of elementary and secondary school teachers. It finds that teacher compensation lags that of workers with similar education and experience, as well as that of workers with comparable skill requirements, like accountants, reporters, registered nurses, computer programmers, clergy, personnel officers, and vocational counselors and inspectors. Incorporating benefits into the analysis does not alter the general picture of teachers having a substantial wage/pay disadvantage that eroded considerably over the last 10 years.

ISBN 1-93-206630-6, 6" x 9", paperback, 76 pages, March 2008, $12.50